MW01222462

PIPE

DREAMS

7 PIPELINES OF CAREER SUCCESS

To Tina —
It was a pleasure meeting you at the ATD Conference. Here's to reaching your potential!

Regards,
Mike

MIKE GELLMAN

Pipe Dreams: 7 Pipelines of Career Success

Copyright © 2014 by Mike Gellman
All rights reserved.

No part of this book may be used or reproduced, stored in a retrieval system, or transmitted in any form or by any means (electronic, mechanical photocopying, recording or otherwise) without the prior written permission of the author.

Published by: CreateSpace Independent Publishing Platform

ISBN-13: 978-1497576568

ISBN-10: 1497576563

Cover design and graphics: Kendra Heard
Book design and additional graphics: Adan M. Garcia, FSi studio
Author profile photos: Susan Manzur, Susan Manzur Photography

Printed in the United States of America.

To my talented young son, Jonas.
My hope for you is to discover and
choose a career path in life that is both
fulfilling and the fullest expression
of your essence and potential.

TABLE OF CONTENTS

FOREWORD

by Anne Shen Smith, former Chairman & CEO of SoCalGas

As the former Chief Executive Officer of the largest natural gas distribution company in the United States and a Board member for a number of community and trade organizations, I have learned many lessons during the 36 years of my career journey.

Mike Gellman articulates an interesting and compelling framework for achieving career advancement and fulfillment, using the model of a gas pipeline system. Both energy industry and non-industry professionals who are striving to get "unstuck" in their careers will benefit from the key principles and thought-provoking questions posed in this small, yet powerful book.

Mike has been a key facilitator of our organization's succession planning process and is a seasoned expert on employee career development. He writes this book based on much experience and personal observations. Mike shares his insights by taking complex yet subtle concepts and presenting them a way that can be easily understood and applied.

Having been in the gas distribution business for all these years, it is fun to see the critical ingredients for career success captured in the framework of a pipeline system. Mike uses analogies such as "maintaining your network of pipes" to describe the need to stay sharp in your skills, and "dealing with corrosion and leaks" to address career setbacks. Mike also covers topics such as the value of having clear purpose and passion, the importance of understanding your personal interests and values, the essentials of being a solid performer, and the requirements for building your potential in the eyes of decision-makers.

Mike goes further to cover ways to prepare for your next steps and contribute your talents to the organization. What I especially like, and hope you do too, are his insights on the dynamics of taking risks, recovering from career detours, and managing the fears encountered along the way.

With the many people I've counseled over the years, the common issues that come up over and over again involve not having a clear and complete picture of what it takes to prepare themselves for success. They have the ambition and the drive to succeed, but lack the understanding of the steps to get there, the powerful organizational dynamics that are at work, and the self-reflection to gauge their personal progress.

I can attest to the powerful influences the factors in *Pipe Dreams: 7 Pipelines of Career Success* have had in my own career journey. During my thirty-six years with Southern California Gas Company, I had the opportunity to work in over a dozen different jobs throughout different areas of the business, each with increasing level of responsibilities and broader sphere of influence. Some of the moves landed me in functions in which I had little experience! The further away from familiar grounds, the greater my anxiety and doubt: Can I learn this job? Can I lead the team to accomplish our goals? Will I succeed? What if I fail? Again and again, I consciously decided to take on personal risks, venture beyond my comfort zone, embrace my fears, then apply all my capacity and energy to learn and excel.

A key lesson from this book is that you are in charge of *your* career. Mike lays out the formula in the book to help you take control of it—beginning with knowing your purpose and passion, then preparation, preferences, principles and values, personality, performance, and potential.

My hope is that you'll dive into this book with an eager mind and courageous heart, and apply the insights to successfully advance your own career.

Sincerely,
Anne Shen Smith
Former Chairman & Chief Executive Officer
Southern California Gas Company

I went to a bookstore and asked the saleswoman, 'Where's the self-help section?' She said if she told me, it would defeat the purpose.

- George Carlin, American
comedian and actor

*P*ipe Dreams: 7 Pipelines of Career Success is composed of three parts. Part I is about **Assessing Your Career Mindset** and includes the Introduction and Chapters 1-3. In the Introduction I share my personal story along with how I came to write this book. Chapter 1 is about understanding *your* personal story and how it influenced where your career is today versus where you want to go. Chapter 2 is about ten common myths that I've found to mislead employees as they navigate their careers. Chapter 3 introduces the **7 Pipelines of Career Success™** model that you can use to better inform and guide your career and avoid the mistakes mentioned in the myths.

Part II is about **Assembling Your Career System.** It consists of Chapters 4-14 that are anchored to and organized around the framework of the pipelines in the **7 Pipelines of Career Success™** model, along with two elements that are also present and interact with the pipes. In the chapters of this section I take you through each of the pipes and elements in the model. First, you will learn about the necessity of getting yourself ready for the journey that you're about to embark on (Chapter 4).

Next, you will learn about how your personal purpose and passion interact with each other to provide you with the direction and energy you need to sustain yourself during your journey (Chapters 5-6). Then we will examine the role that intrinsic factors play in influencing your career choices; your preferences, interests, principles, values, and your personality (Chapters 7-9). We will also examine the implications of your behavior at work—the fundamental feedback needed about your performance that reveals common blind spots that you demonstrate to others (Chapters 10-11). And finally, we will look ahead to possibilities to see how your potential and invisible elements of the model play an important role in your career success and provide the creative space and energy needed for your journey (Chapters 12-14).

In Part III, **Managing Your Career Journey**, I delve into both the internal and external dynamics of career change (Chapters 15-18 and Conclusion). Chapter 15 focuses on navigating *external* resistance and obstacles that you may experience as you work toward building the career you want. As such, you will learn how other people and places may impact your career construction efforts. Next, we'll explore *internal* resistance and obstacles you are likely to experience along the way (Chapters 16-17). These two chapters dive into such internal factors such as fear, taking risks, and how your personal beliefs play a role in making the necessary changes that will allow you to progress toward your career goals. I also discuss the necessary personal care and self-maintenance needed to help sustain you as you manage your career journey using a long-term perspective (Chapter 18). In the Conclusion, the focus is on your future and where to go from here. I encourage you with a "call to action" and the benefits you'll gain by "living" the principles contained in the pipeline model and the rest of this book. Finally, you can refer to the Appendix at the back of this book for brief descriptions and web links to more information about self-awareness tools and resources.

For the most part, the order of these chapters aligns with the order in which they are presented in the model. The model is an integrated system with interdependencies. While the chapters are not fixed to a linear process, the reader will most likely benefit from reading the chapters in sequence since there is some "pipeline logic" to the material in this book. Alternatively, this book can be read in order of the topics that resonate most with you. Although interdependent relationships are called out, each chapter can stand on its own.

For a complimentary Personal Journal Guide to use along with this book, please go to www.7pipelinesofcareersuccess.com.

Sometimes very small investments
can release enormous, infinite
potential that exists in all of us.

- Jacqueline Novogratz, Social entrepreneur
and author of *The Blue Sweater*

PIPE DREAMS

7 PIPELINES OF CAREER SUCCESS

PART I

ASSESSING YOUR CAREER MINDSET

INTRODUCTION

*The future depends on
what we do in the present.*

- Mahatma Ghandi, Leader of the
Indian Independence Movement

MY PIPE DREAM

When I was a kid I wanted to be an Astronomer like Carl Sagan.[1] I was fascinated by the stars in the sky, the Milky Way universe, and the possible worlds and beings beyond our vision. My father arranged for me to borrow a telescope from one of his friends. I remember having that telescope pointed outside my second story bedroom window many nights while I looked at the moon and surrounding stars.

We lived in a modest suburban area of Cleveland where the view was a bit obscured by the city lights, but I was hooked. That is, I was hooked until

---

[1] I've come to realize that many people didn't grow up knowing Carl Sagan as I did. He was a popular American astronomer and author (among his other talents) who had a widely known public television series in the 1980s called "Cosmos: A Personal Voyage."

seventh grade when one of my teachers assigned my class to do career reports. We needed to research a career we were interested in and write a report about it. Naturally, I chose to research careers in Astronomy. Unfortunately, I discovered three very disappointing things:

1. Most Astronomers worked on campuses at universities.
2. Astronomers did not make much money unless you were a famous astronomer like Carl Sagan.
3. To be an Astronomer you needed to know a lot about something called "physics."

I was absolutely crushed! To say the least, these discoveries put a damper on my enthusiasm for becoming an Astronomer. My dream was shattered. I couldn't envision myself being in school any longer than needed—or, especially, working at one! I didn't want to be poor. And I had zero interest in learning about physics. After all, I just wanted to look at the stars and planets in the sky! Becoming a professional Astronomer was not what I originally thought it was.

I am so thankful I got a realistic view of this career to replace my unrealistic, idealized view. From that point on, astronomy became a hobby rather than a career pursuit. It wasn't until high school, after several discussions with a career counselor, plus a human relations class and extracurricular activities, that I realized my interests, true passion and potential were about helping people on a personal level.

Although I had been pretty naïve, I learned a valuable lesson. It pays to take time to get clear on what you want. It pays to do the necessary research and evaluating rather than blindly pursue something you *think* will be what you want.

I was fortunate to have parents who supported me in pursuing what I was passionate about. Many of my peers' parents pressured them to follow in the family footsteps, or to pursue degrees and careers as doctors, lawyers, and other professions that would be worthy of parental pride and approval.

While in graduate school, I was fortunate to work for a local public career center where I facilitated workshops and provided career counseling to clients of diverse backgrounds and work experiences. My clients included laid-off factory workers, full-time housewives who were divorced or widowed, recent college graduates looking for work, mid-career business professionals experiencing challenges finding work, and homeless individuals trying to survive day-to-day.

It was rewarding for me to listen to people's initial stories and then see how they transformed when they were ready to go off in their new directions.

Over the years I made detours in my own career. I explored careers in nonprofit work during a difficult three-year stretch where I shifted from one job to another that was either a temporary position or a regular position that was not a good fit. Eventually, I rediscovered my true strengths and found a more promising path.

As a Sr. Talent Management Advisor for the Southern California Gas Company I have worked with individuals and teams throughout the company to help them work more effectively. I also facilitate succession planning for the organization and launched a highly-regarded Career Coaching & Development Center (CCDC) for the company's employees. It has been a meaningful way for me to make my contribution and to help individuals develop their potential and reach for their dreams.

HOW THIS BOOK CAME TO BE

Over the past several years I commuted many, many miles and hours driving to work by car or taking the train from San Diego and Orange County to Los Angeles and back (sometimes as much as 100-200 miles and three to five hours round-trip several times per week). One day on the train, I was thinking about how nice it is to take the train rather than deal with all the hassles of driving through rush hour traffic—navigating around accidents and fighting off drowsiness early in the morning or after a long day at work. I began thinking about people I help at work who were stressed and unhappy with their careers. Typically, their default reaction was to blame others for their misfortune while overlooking their own responsibility for their situations. They would often ask me, "What's *the* best career path for getting me to XYZ position in this company?" or "I want to become a manager, tell me what I should do." Or "I keep applying and interviewing for jobs, but I can't seem to catch a break."

The important theme I noticed was that my clients consistently were expecting *someone else* to give them the "correct" answer, or to chart their path for them. The reality is that there is no "single" correct path or "one-size-fits-all" approach for your career.

Think about it for a moment. If I drive my car or take the train they both get me to my destination, my workplace. The routes are different, the amount of time it takes to get there is different, the scenery is different, the costs are different, the personal experience is different, and the obstacles are different. Just as there are multiple paths for commuting to work, there are also multiple paths you can take to get the career you want. But you have to figure out what works for you. Otherwise, you're giving your power away to someone else to decide for you. Many people have given away their power to decide about their careers, and they are not happy with the results because they turned over responsibility for personal decisions to someone else.

This book is intended to help you take charge of your career. If you have lost your way or hit a brick wall in your career you can use my pipeline model to get your career on track.

My pipeline model incorporates the most essential components for empowering employees to take charge of their careers rather than gambling on the likelihood of others taking care of them. My sincere wish is that reading this book gives you the knowledge and strategies you need to take charge of your career and realize your career dreams.

Now, on to *your* story!

*All winners of races have this in common –
they dared to cross the starting line.*

- Eliza Rhodes, Writer and philosopher,
author of *Sign Language*

YOUR STORY

There may be many different paths, leading to success – giving up doesn't appear to be one of them.

- Eliza Rhodes, Writer and philosopher, author of *Sign Language*

We all have a story to tell that explains the how, why, and where we are in our careers. Some of us are more reflective and honest with ourselves about where we've been and how we got where we are. Some of us dance around the personal responsibility for choices we've made and we make excuses or blame others for how our work lives have turned out.

As a career coach in both nonprofit and corporate organizations I've heard the angst and helplessness of many dissatisfied and disengaged employees who desperately want to "get ahead" and become happier with their work. The stories I hear come from high-performing individuals who can't seem to "catch a break" and less-noticed employees who silently feel helpless no matter what they do. Some people strongly assert that others have held them back from achieving the satisfaction and success they deserve and want.

There are ten commonly held career myths that employees hold. These are:

1. *If I keep my head down, work hard and perform well, the right person will notice me and tap me on the shoulder for the next great job or opportunity.*

2. *My work speaks for itself.*

3. *My boss doesn't advocate for me to other managers like he or she should.*

4. *The company has no openings or opportunities for career growth.*

5. *It's too late in my career to make a change.*

6. *Everyone should notice how hard I work.*

7. *The most qualified person gets the job.*

8. *There are a "chosen few" who are on the fast track.*

9. *I've been "pigeonholed" or "blacklisted" so I can't go anywhere.*

10. *Taking a step down or making a lateral move will be detrimental to my career.*

Sadly, at one time or another, most of us have subscribed to one of or more of these myths about what it takes to advance our careers within our companies. Too often we carry a mindset of what has been done to us. It is as if there is a play happening all around us and we are in the audience simply watching as our lives unfold before us. While there may be some truth to these myths, they usually fail to tell the whole story.

To complete your story and take ownership of your career it is important to recognize that you are the principal actor in the theater in which you live and work. There may be some "inconvenient truths" tucked away in the recesses of your mind, and perhaps "blind spots," as well (discussed in Chapter 11). However, the more aware you are of your role in the play called "life and work," the more you can direct your career along a more satisfying path.

Pipe Dreams: 7 Pipelines of Career Success is intended to appeal to individuals at all places on the career spectrum, or the "career continuum," as it is often called. Whether you are starting out in your career, somewhere in the middle of your career and starting over, or in the sunset of your career looking to extend your contribution in a meaningful way, my wish is that you will find useful nuggets of wisdom that will improve your particular career situation.

CAREER CONTINUUM

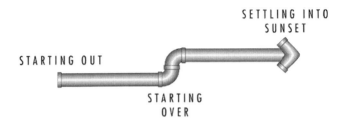

My aim with this book is to provoke new thinking so that you can get unstuck from things that may be unconsciously or consciously limiting your career growth, advancement, satisfaction, and success.

Where are you now? You may be early in your career having recently graduated from college or in a position that is merely a stepping-stone to newer and more exciting opportunities. You may be in the middle of your career and settled into a job that is no longer satisfying. You may be in a job that simply provides a steady income to pay the bills. Or perhaps you are currently straddling the fence wondering whether or not to start over in a new career. Perhaps you are facing retirement within the next five years and carry a strong desire to finish with a flourish or plan for another career (i.e. a sunset career) rather than simply maintain the status quo and slip silently into retirement.

Regardless of where you find yourself, a critical component of a successful and satisfying career is to consciously choose the contributions you want to make. There are many stops along the way, but first it is necessary to better understand the career myths and how they can hold you back from getting to your destination. These myths are the focus of the next chapter.

Questions to consider:

- What's *your* story?
- What part(s) of your story keeps you stuck?
- What myths have you believed at one time or another?
- Where do you fall on the "career continuum?"
- To what extent are you taking charge of your career right now?

If you don't design your own life plan, chances are you'll fall into someone else's plan. And guess what they have planned for you? Not much.

- Jim Rohn, Motivational speaker, entrepreneur and author

LETTING GO OF THE MYTHS

*We have all a better guide
in ourselves, if we would
attend to it, than any
other person can be.*

- Jane Austen, Classic
American novelist

There is silent comfort in holding on to any
one of the myths mentioned in Chapter 1. For
the most part, holding onto myths perpetuates
them and excuses us from taking responsibility
and confronting our own part in the career play
that has unfolded. Unfortunately, holding fast to
myths is likely to be detrimental to your career
and for getting where you want to go.

Sometimes the myths reflect strong cultural
beliefs and attitudes within your family, company
or work team that have gradually been passed on
to influence your thinking. Sometimes there is an
element of truth in each of these myths and it is just

enough to allow them to persist over time despite realities to the contrary.[2]

A common theme among the myths is that career advancement is mostly outside your personal control. Too often people leave it up to a boss, a company, or chance. However, career fulfillment and advancement involve a complex relationship between decisions *you* make and actions *you* take rather than simply what others may do or not do to help you. As humans, when things don't work out the way we want them to, it is easier to blame others than to explore our own role in the results we face. But, it is more beneficial to look at our own assumptions and actions, or non-actions. Let's revisit and tackle these myths one-by-one to better understand the natural appeal they have and the potential consequences of holding on to them.

---

[2]By no means do I claim these ten myths to be all-inclusive. There are many more. My intent is to introduce you to the notion that we all carry different assumptions and beliefs about how things work—our mental frameworks or paradigms—that can hold us back. If you change the stories you tell yourself, you can then begin to change your actions that are based on such stories, and therefore change your outcomes in the direction you desire.

TOP 10 MYTHS

1. *If I keep my head down, work hard and perform well, the right person will take notice and tap me on the shoulder for the next great job or opportunity.*

This is what I refer to as the "good boy" or "good girl" myth. That is, if we follow the rules and do what is expected of us we will be rewarded. While this is admirable—and performing well with a disciplined approach *is* an important aspect of building a career—it is incomplete.

In reality, it's up to you to take the initiative and take charge of your own career. No one is going to care more about you and your interests than you do! If you're waiting to be tapped on the shoulder you may be waiting a long time. In my experience, perhaps only about ten to fifteen percent of employees are selected in this way. Moreover, they have held career conversations with their boss and others, demonstrated initiative, and taken active steps to prepare and position themselves for opportunities that arise. Employees who make themselves, their interests, and their accomplishments known to others are the ones who get what they want.

2. *My work speaks for itself.*

While it is true that the quality of your work speaks volumes about you, this is not a complete picture. Depending on the type of career you aspire to, your current work may or may not illustrate what you're capable of doing in relation to the knowledge, skills, and abilities needed in the wanted position or field. Moreover, if decision-makers are not aware of the work you are doing and its impact on the business, then relying on your work to do the talking for you becomes an ineffective strategy.

3. *My boss doesn't advocate for me to other managers like he or she should.*

There was a time when companies were more paternalistic. Again, no one is going to care more about your career and your development than you. While your boss certainly plays an important role in your career, it is foolish to depend on him or her to pave the way for you. Bosses have their own challenges along with other employees and issues competing for their attention. Your boss may assist you, but ultimately it is up to you to take the initiative and necessary steps to achieve your career goals.

It is worth examining your role here. Does your boss know what your career goals are? How can you help your boss help you? For example, many employees expect their boss to read their minds about what they want and then introduce them to other managers. To complicate things, you may not be clear about what you want to do. Lastly, if your boss has gone out on a limb for you in the past and you turned down an opportunity, the experience may have soured his or her enthusiasm to go through the process again.

4. *The company has no openings or opportunities for career growth.*

People are moving in and out of new or existing positions all the time. For example, there are people going on leave, retiring, moving on to new jobs, and solving both new and long-standing business challenges even in the most sluggish economy or dire company circumstances. It is important to be clear about what you want so you will be able to spot opportunities that are not always obvious to others.

5. *It's too late in my career to make a change at this point.*

Employees regularly tell me they feel they are too old or too far along in their careers to shift gears or go back to school or retrain since they have invested so much in a given career path already. While I can appreciate the sense of overwhelm attached to these concerns, they are self-limiting beliefs that are often perpetuated by erroneous assumptions about what is possible or attainable. Self-limiting beliefs are beliefs that are self-imposed rationalizations or justifications about why something can't be done. There are plenty of people who have reinvented themselves in their later years. Likewise, there are many people early in their careers who have set aside freshly-minted degrees to pursue careers more in line with their passions.

6. *Everyone should notice how hard I work.*

Everyone is also busy doing his or her own thing. Being a hard worker is frequently not sufficient for getting noticed, particularly if you don't get results. In fact, "working hard" is typically expected of everyone and not necessarily the strongest distinguishing factor. Moreover, some employees work very hard, but are not efficient or do not follow through as promised, or they repeat a lot of the same mistakes or take too long to achieve their results.

7. *The most qualified person gets the job.*

There are underlying assumptions here. One is that everyone is aware of the most qualified person, and another is that there is a common understanding of what "most qualified" means.

Also, qualified people may not show up as hiring managers expected. That is, a hiring manager may have a person in mind for a position, but the person may not be interested in the opportunity. Sometimes the most qualified candidate is interested in an available opportunity but the timing for a change is not right, as when a manager has a valued employee who is needed until a critical project is completed. It is also possible that a most qualified candidate may have more than one job offer at the same time. Finally, some employees may have all the "technical" qualifications but they lack other attributes that are equally, if not more, important.

8. There's a "chosen few" who are on the fast track.

While there certainly are employees who have caught the attention of decision-makers, there is no reason why you can't get on their radar screen and better position yourself for current and future opportunities, too. It is in a company's best interest to have a strong pool of employees to draw upon for filling critical needs. It is important to be visible, build a strong network, and be known to others; yet those are not the only criteria. Other factors such as your performance, intelligence, judgment, reputation, drive, personality, attitude, enthusiasm, cultural fit, and potential are also important.

9. I've been "pigeonholed" or "blacklisted" so I can't go anywhere.

In all honesty, many employees are their own worst enemies. They tell themselves a story about how they have been pigeonholed or blacklisted, and either typecast or marked with a "scarlet letter"[3] of sorts. If you have been doing the same type of work or you have been in the same job for a long period of time it is not uncommon to feel stuck or typecast because that is all other people believe you can do. Likewise, you may think you have been blacklisted or unfairly prevented from future career opportunities if you annoyed or left a bad impression on a hiring manager during your career. Not only can this subconsciously affect your performance, but your attitude can suffer as well. Employees adopt a feeling of helplessness and a "why should I even try" attitude. This in turn creates a self-fulfilling prophecy where performance stagnates or drops and the output is negative energy. A proactive approach, then, is to make your desires clear, to be open to feedback, and to ask which attributes and skills are required to obtain the desired position.

---

[3]A scarlet letter is a symbol of shame that was derived from Nathaniel Hawthorne's classic romance novel about a fictional character named Hester Pryne who had an adulterous affair. As part of the punishment for her crime she was forced to wear a large "A" on her dress while in public for all to see.

10. *Taking a step down or making a lateral move will be detrimental to my career.*

The career landscape is different now and advancing does not always involve moving up. Climbing the corporate ladder is not the most appropriate paradigm any longer. It is more beneficial to look at career opportunities as a lattice that has both vertical and horizontal paths. Many executives and managers within companies did not take a straight path to get to their senior positions. Like a lattice, many moved sideways, diagonally, down, over, and up in order to learn the business and pick up new skills needed to achieve their career goals. Furthermore, many employees do not want to be in a role where they are managing others; they would rather develop a sense of mastery in a technical field.

By broadening your thinking about what career advancement means, you are likely to discover previously unseen opportunities and options. Subsequently, it is up to you to determine which ones best support your career goals.

For you to get "unstuck" in your career it is important to examine some of your beliefs. If you found that you subscribe to any of the above myths, I encourage you to take a closer look at why you cling to them.

Questions to consider:

- How many of these myths apply to you?
- What has your part been in perpetuating these myths?
- How would you have managed your career differently if you had known all along these myths weren't true?

*Unless someone like you cares
a whole awful lot, nothing is
going to get better. It's not.*

- Dr. Seuss, Beloved children's
book author

THE 7 PIPELINES OF CAREER SUCCESS™ MODEL

You don't have to be great to start,
but you have to start to be great.

- Zig Ziglar, Author and
motivational speaker

Most clients who come to me are seeking some form of advice, support or guidance. Either they are unhappy with their current career situation or they are eager to take things to the next level and want to take advantage of best practices used by others who have succeeded. My clients have a lot of questions about what they should do. They bring a mix of strong emotions and experiences with them. They most commonly struggle with where to start and the best course of action to follow.

This book provides a framework to help you move forward on your career journey. I created a model, the **7 Pipelines of Career Success**™ to explain the essential components. I will briefly explain the components of the model and then we will explore each of them in upcoming chapters so you can apply the information to your own situation.

7 PIPELINES OF CAREER SUCCESS™ MODEL

The **7 Pipelines of Career Success**™ model was born out of the recognition that many factors come together to serve as a catalyst for your growth. This model is composed of seven pipes and two elements. The pipes are Purpose and Passion, Preparation, Preferences, Principles and Values, Personality, Performance, and Potential. In addition, there are two important elements, Space and Energy, which interact with these pipes. Although invisible, these elements are present. What follows is a brief description of each component of the Pipeline model.

PURPOSE AND PASSION

The largest pipe is at the heart of the model: *Purpose and Passion*. It is essential to understand the "why" and the "what" behind the career journey you are about to embark upon so you will have sufficient motivation to take the trip. Identifying your "calling," or reason for being, helps to visualize an ideal destination for your career journey. The tension between where you are now and where you want to be provides the motivation to take the trip in the first place. Understanding what you are passionate about helps inform the means by which you get to your destination. This understanding also serves as an internal compass to inform you when you are on the right path versus when you are straying towards an undesirable path.

PREPARATION

The second pipe is *Preparation*. Before you can begin your career journey, you must get ready for it so you can increase the likelihood of getting where you want to go. Otherwise, you will likely end up wandering aimlessly, or circling round and round and getting nowhere fast. Proper preparation will help set you up for the best chances for success.

PREFERENCES

The third pipe is *Preferences*. Identifying your preferences is about understanding the activities you would choose to do without the interference of others who may want something different for you. Preferences are also known as interests. Your preferences are signals of what your underlying needs are. Becoming clear on your preferences can inform you about how you want to experience your day-to-day reality and what choices will be most satisfying for your career.

PRINCIPLES/VALUES

The fourth pipe is *Principles and Values*. These are your fundamental beliefs and indicate what is most important to you in life your relationships with others and yourself. Although many people are consciously unaware when their underlying principles and values are at play in day-to-day situations, these are core motivators in our daily actions and choices. They are part of who we are. Values are activated and rise to the surface when there are tough choices to make in any situation.

PERSONALITY

The fifth pipe is *Personality*. Your personality is an expression of who you are and how others experience you. Personalities are varied just as jobs are varied. Both have innate characteristics that interact with each other in positive and negative ways. Knowing how your personality is suited for potential opportunities is an essential component of finding a satisfying fit for you.

PERFORMANCE

The sixth pipe is *Performance*. Your performance in any job is a critical indicator about how well-suited you are for a given job or career, but it also opens the door to future opportunities. With solid performance and a strong track record, you will typically have greater access to opportunities than someone who performs poorly in their job.

POTENTIAL

The seventh pipe is *Potential*. One of our greatest allies for career success rests in the inherent potential we hold to become more than what we are today. Your career potential is an amalgamation of your capacity for learning and growing into your future self. Building and demonstrating your potential is one of the best things you can do for opening the door to career goals that you wish to reach.

SPACE

In addition to the seven pipes above, there are two important elements. *Space* is the first element in the Pipeline model. The notion of space plays an important role in your ability to operate effectively and be flexible and creative in your job. Space includes the ability to prevent or absorb unexpected circumstances, and the capacity to take advantage of new opportunities as they arise.

ENERGY

Energy is the second element in the Pipeline model. You need sufficient motivation to sustain you and help you get where you want to go. Purpose and Passion play a big role in that, as does satisfying your preferences and underlying needs. The extent to which you are able to get or to generate the necessary energy to sustain you during your career journey will help you make it to your desired career destination.

In the following chapters, we will take a deeper look at each pipe and element and how each one fits together.

Questions to consider:

- Which pipes or elements are strongest for you?
- Which pipes or elements need the greatest amount of attention from you?

I challenge you today to find a passion or cause for you today...and know that you can make a difference. You can make change because you're part of the group that would rather light candles than curse the darkness and that glow will fill the world.

- Leigh Steinberg, Sports agent and inspiration for the film *Jerry Maguire*

PART II

MANAGING YOUR CAREER JOURNEY

CHART YOUR PURPOSE

*The place God calls you to is the
place where your deep gladness
and the world's deep hunger meet.*

- Frederick Beuchner, Theologian
and author of *Wishful Thinking:
A Seeker's ABC*

Just as you are attempting to move your career
from where you are now to where you wish
to be, parallels can be drawn from the pipeline
operation. Let's take a closer look and examine
the similarities.

The purpose of a gas distribution system is to move fuel from point A to point B while ensuring the consistent delivery of gas to customers who depend on this resource to heat their homes and workplaces, cook their food, and light up their lives. When there is a rupture in the pipeline and gas can no longer safely reach customers, the damaged pipe gets closed off and a series of back-up pipes step in and maintain gas flow in order to maintain the system's performance and uninterrupted service to customers.

The system has a defined purpose, a clear reason for being in existence—and it has a significant impact on people's daily lives. Yet, when working properly, the system typically goes unnoticed to customers. A pipeline without a clear purpose quickly loses value, so, just as it would be ridiculous to build a pipeline without an end-customer in mind, it is absurd to build your career without an end-goal in mind.

Sometimes gas service is taken for granted. When a water heater goes out or the gas range is off kilter, people notice what is missing right away. The value is there all along whether people are aware of it or not. When a house burns down, the pipes are still underground and may temporarily be without purpose. Once a house is rebuilt, the value of the pipes increases.

Similarly, you also have a purpose and inherent value: You have a reason for your existence. You have something important to offer the company and community you live and work in. In fact, they both "miss out" when your contributions are absent. Often, your purpose becomes clouded by the daily activities and stressors of life that draw your attention away from your core or true understanding and connection with yourself.

Your house is analogous to your career. Your personal pipes are at the core of who you are. Therefore, you (and your career) still have value when you are burned out, at a dead-end job, or laid off. Your personal pipes are still connected to other facets of your life; your family, friends, spirituality, health, etc. As you rebuild your career the value of who you are becomes more evident to yourself and to others.

YOUR VISION OF CAREER SUCCESS

We often measure our value by whether or not we have been "successful" at work and life. But, what is success? The definition of career success varies for each person. The ways you define and envision your success are important ideas worth delving deeply into.

Having a personal vision is like a dream that incorporates your deepest desires. It is a future state in time; five, ten, twenty, thirty years or more. It encompasses the legacy that you want to create and how you want to experience your career and life. It's a picture to be painted:

- What do you see in the picture?
- Who is in the picture?
- What are you doing or what have you done?
- What does it feel like to be in that future place?
- What has been your contribution or impact during that period of time?

The strategies available to make your vision a reality will either be limited or expanded depending on how you define your vision. You may define success as achieving a promotion to a prominent position, or status within the company or community in which you work or live. Likewise, you may be financially motivated and define success by how much money you make. Alternatively, you can define success by your ability to balance demands of work and home, and doing what you love to do while leveraging your strengths. Finally, there might not be anything more important to you than having a positive impact on other people's lives in some way, or having a meaningful impact on your community.

In order to expand the potential strategies for achieving success, it is helpful to take a step back and develop a clearer picture of what you want to achieve. Not only that, I have seen over and over how my clients feel liberated when they take time to reflect and to examine what success means to them.

How you define success plays an important role in how you "show up" on life's stage. This consciously and unconsciously shapes your career journey along the way. It enables the choices and decisions you make each day, both small and large, as well as the actions you take or choose not to take.

INSIDE INSIGHT

The Power of Vision

Before I first began working for the energy industry, I had gone through a challenging three-year period in my career where I kept finding myself in work environments that were abusive and crazy-making. Much of the time I felt like I had lost my bearings, so I set aside some time to take stock of what I really wanted for myself. I ended up writing a two-page narrative describing what type of work I wanted to be doing, the impact it would have on others, what kind of coworkers I would be working with, and how I would experience my work life. I created a vision for my future that included working for a nonprofit, biotech, or consulting firm.

A couple years later, I came across that journal entry. My jaw dropped as I read what I had written. What I had described as what I wanted in my vision was something that I was actually living. Ninety-percent had become a reality without me realizing it. I had never even had utilities on my radar; in fact, I thought they were "boring and bureaucratic." To my amazement, I had landed in a place that was definitely not that—it had the great leadership I wanted, talented colleagues, a creative and collaborative environment, a flexible work schedule, and a compensation package that enabled me to pay the bills and save for my son's and my own future.

What do you see when you close your eyes and concentrate on your personal vision?

YOUR CAREER MISSION

To the extent that you are able to develop a clear vision of what success looks like and why you want it, you can then begin to think about how you want to go about achieving it. Similar to the core purpose of a natural gas pipeline system, the way in which you want to go about achieving success is informed by your core purpose, why you exist.

Your purpose answers the question "why?" and is closely intertwined with goals. A personal vision with goals provides direction, while purpose provides the reason for moving in that direction. Understanding your purpose is a step in creating your personal blueprint or map.

Clarity of purpose, otherwise known as your personal mission or your calling, enables you to plan your career route and design your system in a way that will enable you to deliver and contribute what you do best. It helps you chart desired inputs (contributions) and outputs (legacy) and a direction to move toward. Therefore, it is important to understand where are you now (part A) and where you want to be (part B).

CAREER BLUEPRINT

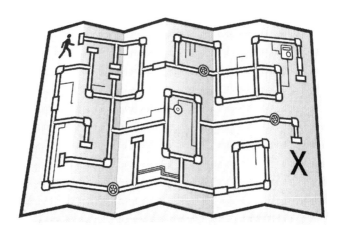

One of the secrets for clarifying your purpose is to become more aware about what is important to you and to tune into what you are passionate about. In fact, this is the subject of the next chapter, *Discover Your Passion*.

The following questions will help you clarify your purpose and support the development of your road map to a new or updated definition of success.

Questions to consider:

- Why do you exist? What might your purpose be?
- What do you envision for your future?
- How do *you* define success? What does it look and feel like?
- What types of achievements and/or impacts do you yearn to achieve in your lifetime?
- What value or contribution do you *want* to provide to others?

> *There is one quality which one must possess to win, and that is definiteness of purpose, the knowledge of what one wants, and a burning desire to possess it.*

> - Napoleon Hill, Author of
> *Think and Grow Rich*

DISCOVER YOUR PASSION

*It is your passion that empowers
you to be able to do that thing
you were created to do.*

- T.D. Jakes, Influential
religious leader

A key strength in an effective career is knowing
yourself and having a clear understanding of what
energizes you and brings forth your best self. You will
be an asset contributing your maximum value to your
company when you are passionately engaged.

The maintenance of the gas transmission and distribution system takes a lot of heart and soul, relentless care about safety, getting the product to customers reliably, and keeping costs low. People notice when there is a sense of pride and when employees are engaged and demonstrating a high level of commitment to the organization, its mission and its customers. Even more, people take notice of the dedication and extraordinary efforts that are made during crises such as natural disasters, and when unforeseen challenges or complications arise. Passion breathes life into the pipeline system like air. When a pipeline is fully engaged and fully utilizing the capacity it has available, it is contributing maximum value as an asset.

When people consistently demonstrate excess capacity available and offer discretionary effort to volunteer by going the extra mile and exceeding expectations, it gets noticed and recognized by leaders throughout an organization. When you display such passion and extra effort those around you will positively experience you as having a can-do attitude and the right work ethic. In effect, one of the main outputs or by-products of "living your passion" is the increased visibility gained from decision-makers who can positively affect your career. Moreover, passion ultimately is at the heart of your *sustained* career success.

When passion is absent, growth can become stagnant, work can feel more laborious, and you increase your risk of becoming burned out.

INSIDE INSIGHT

Pipeliners: Arrogant or Passionate?

Pipeline operations employees, aka "Pipeliners," those who physically work on and operate the pipelines, are among the most dedicated employees I've encountered in the gas business. When I first started facilitating succession planning within the gas industry, I quickly became aware of this particular group of employees who seemed to be a lightning rod for controversy in the organization. Some colleagues and clients described pipeliners as if they were a different breed than other employees. In fact, there were often disputes between pipeline operations employees and other groups about their relative importance to the organization. Some folks viewed pipeliners as being "arrogant" and acting as if they thought they were better than everyone else. Other folks viewed them as "dedicated" and recognized the critical role of their function within the pipeline operation.

Regardless of which perspective was held about the pipeliners, no one denied they were ultra-passionate about the work they did for the company.

This is not to say that other groups of employees weren't incredibly passionate as well. However, pipeline operations employees have a specialization that other people, inside and outside the company, typically don't know much about or understand. They mostly work behind the scenes. They work on the pipelines that transport gas from the source and funnel it to other parts of the gas system where it will eventually be delivered to homes and businesses. Pipeliners' jobs are highly dangerous and they know it. Although they are typically unseen, the entire system rides on whether or not they perform their jobs well. They know this too.

The point is this: Passion is essential. Pipeliners' passion for what they do, and their understanding of how their work fits into the big picture, sustains them, even during crisis situations. Their sense of duty and commitment demonstrates a combination of purpose and passion that enables them to perform at high levels. As such, they typically perform safely and reliably no matter what time of day it may be, how tired they may get, or what obstacles they may face.

> *What activities or causes are you so passionate about that you are willing to persevere and maintain focus in the face of challenges while others may simply give up?*

A PASSION-PURPOSE PUNCH

Stirring passion and purpose together creates something new and powerful. Too much of one or the other, or the absence of one or the other, leads to poor results. When the correct mixture of air and gas is combined, it creates optimal conditions for the productive release of energy that enables people to heat their homes and businesses, and operate their lives day to day.

Similarly, the appropriate mixture of passion and purpose creates the optimal conditions for your career success. Passion also provides the necessary air for breathing life into your success. Heated up, air expands. Likewise, heating up your passion expands your capacity for standing out, getting noticed, adding discretionary value to the company and advancing your career.

Passion and purpose are inextricably intertwined. Passion without purpose may generate a lot of activity, yet may take you on tangents that do not move you toward your desired destination, your vision. Over time, this condition creates a hit-or-miss scenario where going "off-track" becomes the norm and reaching your destination is simply the product of dumb luck.

PASSION-PURPOSE PUNCH

On the other hand, purpose without passion is a fruitless pursuit—a checkbox item without the joy of getting there. Purpose without passion may steer you in the right direction toward your destination, but you won't enjoy the journey to get there. Passion will help sustain you when obstacles are placed in your path. Identifying your purpose and passion can be challenging. However, it's worth investing the time and energy to identify both of them. Together, passion and purpose form a powerful one-two punch.

When passion is present, it can have a multiplier effect. As implied in the burned-down house scenario in the previous chapter on *Chart Your Purpose,* a pipeline without a house attached has less value than one with a connected house. People who live in a house can benefit from what the pipeline has to offer. An employee with purpose, but without much passion, has diminished value. Passion connects to everything else you do somewhat like a rising tide that lifts all boats.

For instance, passion positively influences other dimensions such as your performance and potential—two pipes in the model that we will visit later in this book. With all the pressures of day-to-day living you may struggle to see what you are passionate about and you rely on others to tell you what you should do. In my experience, clients who identify their own source of passion achieve more sustainable results and greater sense of satisfaction with their work in the long run. That is, no one can "give" you your passion. It is intrinsic to you. Therefore, it is internally derived instead of derived externally from someone else.

Where does passion come from? Passion is derived from many sources. Your passion may be hidden away and trapped under the surface or diluted within your work environment. In the pipeline business natural gas can come from a variety of places such as underground caverns, shale, and cow flatulence. Just like gas rises, passion rises within people. With people, passion comes from within and rises up naturally when given sufficient space to do so. You do not have to "work at it" when you are tapping your natural source of energy. What are the sources of your passion?

UNTAPPED RESOURCES

In the pipeline industry there are areas where natural gas is typically found, and unusual areas, too. Sometimes there are areas that are known and they are easily accessible. Other times, the areas are known but gas cannot be tapped into for political, social, legal, moral or technological reasons. Similarly, there are times when factors interfere with your ability to draw upon some of your passions.

For example, let's say that you are passionate about solving challenging problems. You notice that a process you use in your department is inefficient and plagued with redundancies. Perhaps your manager expects you to keep the established procedures of your position rather than spend time creating alternatives. If you know what your passion is, what is preventing or stopping you from tapping into it?

Furthermore, natural gas can lie stagnant and undetected in underground storage caverns, between layers of bedrock, and pipelines just as your passions can lie stagnant and undetected. In the energy industry, even once gas is found, there is typically a lengthy process for accessing it and transporting it to customers because a series of steps must occur over a period of time. Likewise, you will find that you need to take several steps to identify and clarify your passions and apply them at work.

Here are some additional circumstances that may play into why you are not tapping into your passion:

- You lack awareness of what your true passion is.
- You feel social pressure that discourages expression of your passion, such as family, other workers or company culture.
- You were told it will never pay much nor be a good choice to pursue.
- Your current job does not provide an opportunity to demonstrate your passion.
- You don't know how to access and apply your passion.

When stored properly, natural gas can serve as a strategic reserve. This reserve enables operators to draw upon it in the future when needed to buffer customers against high market prices or conditions with limited availability of gas on the open market. If not monitored correctly however, gas pressure can build to dangerous levels and lead to negative consequences such as soil contamination, or perhaps an explosion.

Like gas, your passion will naturally and eventually build pressure over time. Eventually your state of mind is likely to be negatively affected if there is no outlet for your passion. Just as pipeline operators need to get things in place before building or making changes to a system, it makes sense for you to adequately prepare for your career journey so you can be ready to "live" your passion and "fulfill" your purpose. The next chapter, *Prepare To Get What You Want*, discusses factors to consider as you embark on your career journey.

Questions to consider:

- How engaged are you at work and in life?
- What steps might you take to discover and release your passion?
- How are you impacting others when you're working at your best?
- How do you feel about yourself when working at your best (when you're "in the flow")?
- What are the personal consequences of storing your passion and energy but not tapping into it?

I am a song. I live to be sung.
I sing with all my heart!

- John Denver, Singer,
songwriter and poet

PREPARE TO GET
WHAT YOU WANT

If you don't know where you're going,
you'll end up someplace else.

- Yogi Berra, Baseball Hall-of-
Famer and philosopher

Any large pipeline system consists of a series of complex interconnected pipes that work together to deliver a product to customers. Your career is similar because there are also numerous interconnected dimensions of your life that need to blend together to create and move you toward your compelling future. Determining what you want your future to look and feel like, and how you will get there, takes time and a thoughtful approach.

Designing, constructing and maintaining a large network of pipelines requires careful and thoughtful planning, as well. These three phases are sometimes referred to as pre-construction, build, and post-construction. Much preparation needs to happen before, during, and after just about any pipe is laid in the ground. Your career planning has equivalent phases, too.

The three construction phases include activities such as demand and growth forecasting, identifying overarching goals and objectives, mapping proposed routes for laying pipes, conducting environmental impact studies, estimating construction costs, securing right-of-way permits and regulatory approvals, negotiating contracts, ordering necessary pipeline materials, etc. Meanwhile, there are always unanticipated situations and circumstances that emerge.

Similar to the three phases of construction of a pipeline, there are important activities and tasks for you to keep in mind before, during, and after potential career opportunities arise. For example, you will need to conduct your own research, be mindful of company procedures and politics, and ideally obtain permission or support from your boss to interview for other opportunities in the company, and then negotiate your salary and working conditions. Adequate preparation will position you to identify and take advantage of opportunities as they arise. To the extent that you invest the necessary time to plan how you will build your career, you will also increase your chances of having a more rewarding and successful one.

There is more to consider, however. Each day it takes a high level of planning to efficiently dispatch field personnel to service customers' needs. Dozens of personnel in fleet trucks are dispatched to turn on or turn off gas at homes or businesses, troubleshoot gas leaks, fix damaged pipes, or lay new pipes. When working well, the routes that field technicians and their fleet of trucks follow to get from one job to the next are optimized to reduce unnecessary trips, overlapping territories, and circling back to neighborhoods where they were earlier in the day.

Ideally, routes are planned and mapped out ahead of time to operate efficiently. In reality, dispatch personnel and the specialized software used to make choices about best routes sometimes make poor choices because they lack up-to-date information on road construction, closed streets, etc.

Likewise, you may not have all the pertinent information you need for your career journey.

Very rarely will your career follow a planned and mapped-out route to where you want to go, even when you know where you are going. When field personnel encounter a closed road it may take longer to get to the customer, and this can create a chain of events impacting everyone. It is similar for your career in the sense that it may take longer to reach your destination when you encounter unexpected delays and obstacles.

Just as with field personnel and their dispatchers, you may have been reliant on others to make choices for you and your career path. Many people end up in a career influenced by pressure from family, culture or other circumstances. Perhaps one or more of the following circumstances influenced you:

- Your parents wanted you to follow in their footsteps.
- Your economic or cultural upbringing dictated choices available to you.
- You stumbled into your career by accident.
- You dreamed of the career you are in and then realized later it was not what you thought it was.
- You are ready for a mid-career change after the flame has burned out on your current one.

INSIDE INSIGHT

How Family and Culture Influenced One Client's Definition of Success

I was working with a client several years ago, "Sunni" (not her real name), who was determined to get promoted to a manager position. She was a highly intelligent woman in a male-dominated profession (she was a software programmer) and she made it very clear to her boss and others that she deserved to be promoted. The problem was that her boss felt she wasn't performing to his expectations, while project managers she indirectly reported to outside his department complained that she was non-compliant, she produced work that was sub-par quality, and she challenged them at almost every turn.

When coaching her, I explored her reasons for wanting to become a manager. It turns out the main reason she was so adamant about being a manager was related to the family dynamics and culture she grew up in. She told me that people in her culture didn't view individuals as being successful unless they attained some level of stature such as manager. Even if she had been a stellar performer in her current role she wouldn't have been considered a success. Sunni was stuck.

Therein lies a common challenge among individuals building their careers. Sunni was using other people's yardsticks rather than her personal yardstick to measure her own success. Although she enjoyed mentoring others who were junior to her, she lacked the necessary skills to be a manager. After probing more with her, it was clear that she didn't relish the idea of managing people and budgets. She only wanted the title and more pay.

If you were coaching her, what would you advise and why?

Regardless of how you got where you are, there is something positive to be gained from all of your work experiences. Whether you realize it or not there is inherent value in all the twists and turns and detours you made in your career. The good news is that you've been preparing your whole life for your next great opportunity. The payoff comes when you invest the time to better understand yourself and dig up the common themes that are woven throughout your life's journey so that you can discover potential career opportunities.

Sometimes you can create your own opportunities. Be aware of what will best position you to take advantage of opportunities as they arise. Developing an acute awareness of your overarching goals and objectives provides clues about what you have been preparing for in the future. Your task here is to develop the big picture. You can start developing your big picture by looking at and evaluating themes from your past and current experiences and exploring how they relate to the other pipelines in the **7 Pipelines of Career Success™** model.

When factored together, you can maximize the benefits of the **7 Pipelines of Career Success™** by leveraging the "Four A's of Preparation." These Four A's involve a continuous cycle of deepening levels of awareness which include:

1. *Assessing* yourself.

2. *Analyzing* your strengths and opportunities.

3. Taking *Action* to develop and promote yourself.

4. *Attracting* what you want.

STEP 1. ASSESS

First, assess yourself! In the pipelines business, smart sensors and meters can provide feedback about system performance and alert operators to things gone astray, such as notifications about changes in pipeline pressure during an earthquake. Similarly, it is powerful to be aware of your strengths, development needs, and blind spots. The essence of this step is to take stock of yourself and have a holistic perspective of where you are, who you are, and what you value so you can begin to develop a personal vision and mission for what you want and where you want to go.

- Do you have a clear sense of what matters most to you?
- Are you willing to explore and examine weaknesses that could potentially be fatal flaws?
- Do you have people or processes to evaluate and provide you with feedback on how you show up at work?

STEP 2. ANALYZE

Next, analyze your strengths and opportunities in relation to your current career and your desired or ideal career. Understanding your work environment is important. In the pipeline business, there are certain criteria that provide the most favorable conditions or environment for laying down a series of pipes. These include having community support, clear right-of-way, favorable regulatory and economic circumstances, easy access to needed materials and skilled labor, and more.

Ultimately, pipeline operators need to determine whether or not the company's goal is feasible. They will ask themselves whether or not the project will be a cost-effective and acceptable route to lay the pipes, and if it can be built on time and on budget. Essentially, they want to determine if there is a match or alignment between the company's interests and needs and the interest and needs of the communities that will be affected by the project.

Developing a clear set of your own criteria from which to evaluate potential opportunities can be a lifesaver and will ensure alignment with your personal mission and vision. There must also be alignment between you and your company's culture, needs, interests, values, as well as skills and potential. Analyze for fit by comparing your assets to both your team's andcompany's needs and culture. The essence of this step is to identify the type of work and work environment that will be the *best fit* for you. The greater the overlap, the better the fit.

- What is your assessment of your company or team's culture? What are acceptable and non-acceptable practices?
- To what degree are your interests and strengths a good fit for what your company values and needs, either now or in the near future?
- Will your weaknesses be a factor or not? If so, how can you shore them up or manage around them?

STEP 3. ACT

The third step in the process is to identify what actions are necessary to focus on for your development and visibility. Many employees have this mindset: *"If I work hard, keep my nose to the grindstone and perform well, people will notice my good work and I'll get promoted or tapped on the shoulder for special projects."* While that does occur occasionally, it is typically not how people advance—especially in large organizations.

We are not in a paternalistic business environment anymore. Today this is an increasingly diminishing cultural norm in organizations. Therefore, this reality requires a shift in how you view responsibility for your career advancement. You need to have a mindset of taking matters into your own hands. Do key decision-makers know of your career interests? Those who advance make their interests known and they volunteer for special projects, assignments, and jobs that stretch them or play to their strengths.

You are the chief engineer of your own career! Once you recognize that you are in the driver's seat rather than the passenger's seat, you have a number of actions you can take. Some effective strategies include scheduling a career conversation with your boss, networking and building relationships with others in your company, conducting informational interviews[4] with individuals in fields and jobs that interest you, volunteering for a cross-functional team or committee, taking on a stretch assignment, pursuing lateral moves or temporary assignments in a new area, and turning around a struggling project to name a few.

In essence, you are attempting to better position yourself in the sea of other employees in your organization. As you promote yourself and gain momentum based on our actions, you naturally begin to take greater ownership and influence over your career. Act as if you are serious about getting a new career. These steps will help you develop greater visibility among leaders in your company and enable

---

[4]Not to be confused with a job interview, an informational interview is an informal method of interviewing someone for information. This conversation helps you research information and "pick someone's brain" about a job, career, company, or industry that you are interested in learning more about. It is an excellent research and networking tool for helping you get a better understanding or "inside scoop" to help you with your career planning, assessing potential fit, or simply expanding your knowledge about a given area.

you to shape and promote your personal brand. Your brand includes your reputation and how well you live up to it. There will be more about personal branding in Chapter 13, *Build Your Potential.*

- How can you increase your visibility? Who needs to know more about you, your career aspirations and learn what you have to offer?
- What opportunities are there to increase your personal network and strengthen relationships?
- How can you contribute to your company and maximize your discretionary effort in ways that will support your "career campaign?"

STEP 4. ATTRACT

The fourth step is to attract what you want. The energy generated from taking ownership radiates outward. Your intentions send a signal to others about who you are, and they work like an electro-magnet to attract what you want. In the energy industry, or any industry for that matter, a company's steadfast commitment to living its core values, purpose, and vision naturally draws individuals who share and support these attributes.

Likewise, if you put out energy that signals what you want, the "universe" will answer.[5] How? Your purpose and passion become woven into your conversations, the actions you take, and the choices you make to help you move closer toward your goal; consciously and unconsciously. When you have clarity of purpose and bridge together the essentials, the universal laws of attraction will be at work. People will sense your enthusiasm and energy.

It is important to be passionate and stay true to your core values, purpose, and vision and ask for what you want. Often called "making the ask," this is a way to let other people know how they can help you. It gives others an understanding of what you are striving for and is like planting seeds in soil. Your enthusiasm and energy act as natural fertilizers. Eventually, the right people will respond and help you along your career journey.

- What kinds of career opportunities do you want to attract?
- What attention and opportunities have you typically attracted over the years?

---

[5]Yes, I admit this may sound "new agey" and esoteric. This line of thinking is based on a dynamic in quantum physics called the "law of attraction." Other variations of this principle include "karma" or what "goes around, comes around," or "you get what you give" or "you reap what you sow." Basically, if you keep putting out positive energy, eventually others will listen, feel, and respond to it, and you will reap positive outcomes in return.

Have they been positive or negative experiences?

- What must happen first to begin attracting what you want or more of what you want in your career?

Here is how the four A's come together to prepare you for your next great opportunity: When you are clear about who you are and what you want (assess) and how that relates to the company you work for (analyze) while taking proactive steps to move toward what you want (act), you will ultimately draw in the types of career opportunities that perhaps were previously unknown (attract).

A place to start planning your career journey is to take a look at your preferences. These are activities and choices you make on a day-to-day basis that provide helpful indicators and tangible signals about which routes you might take. The next chapter, *Survey Your Preferences*, further delves into clarifying what you want, understanding available options, and matching them to the right opportunities.

> *If you don't design your own life plan,*
> *chances are you'll fall into someone*
> *else's plan. And guess what they*
> *have planned for you? Not much.*
>
> - Jim Rohn, Entrepreneur and author

CHAPTER 7

SURVEY YOUR PREFERENCES

The more I want to get something done, the less I call it work.

- Richard Bach, Author of
Jonathan Livingston Seagull

Understanding your preferences can be described as who you would choose to be, what you would choose to say and do, and how you would choose to live your life without any external pressure or influence. Understanding your preferences also provides important clues about what energizes and motivates you. As such, preferences consist of both interests *and* underlying needs and motivators.

Preferences encompass career interests. These interests are revealed by patterns of choices you make over a period of time. Of these choices, people typically gravitate toward work using their head, heart, or hands.

For example, you may prefer to focus on systems, procedures, and operating standards. Others may prefer to work with less tangible aspects of jobs such as imagining or brainstorming ideas and designing, called using your head. If you prefer to focus on the tangible, physical or technical aspects of a job you are typically using your hands. If you prefer to focus on relationships by engaging, influencing, and motivating people then you are using your heart.

Let's take a look at how this notion of preferences plays out in the pipeline business. Preferences within a natural gas delivery system can include an array of items including certain pipefitting materials, fleet vehicles, fuel mixture, communications equipment, and informational technology. Underlying needs are made to serve our interests related to such things as quality, safety, reliability, functionality, and flexibility. These preferences, or interests are inherently rooted in the tasks that need to be performed and the desired outcomes they are intended or designed to achieve.

Employees in a pipeline business have personal preferences related to operating their part of the pipeline. Field personnel and engineers will have different personal preferences about their work. Their different choices naturally lead to different sets of career options.

In the pipeline business, many employees who come into construction related jobs usually begin their careers in entry level positions such as meter readers. Historically, most meter readers tend to be younger employees who are recent high school graduates, college students, or in the process of enrolling in college. Once they prove themselves as meter readers they have more options to follow their preferences.

Generally, meter readers have two main career paths. Some opt to become energy technicians repairing appliances in people's homes. Alternatively, they can choose to do field work along the pipelines as construction technicians digging ditches with shovels and laying pipe.

There are tradeoffs to consider. The work environment of a construction technician involves more physical work, whereas the energy technician deals with more complex problem-solving and customer relations. If construction technicians discover that operating shovels and jackhammers is not a good fit, they can apply for energy technician positions. As they get more seniority they may become technical leads or supervisors.

These are the basic career paths available to them. If these career choices do not match an employee's preferences, it will be necessary to obtain more education for moving to other roles in the company.

On the other hand, employees with a college degree have different career paths than meter readers. They usually have more job options. For example, an engineer starting with a company can work in either an office or field setting, and will have greater autonomy over the work and have a wider variety of assignments. Another choice will be to move into a leadership role or remain in a technical role as an individual contributor.

Typically, engineers are more interested in "head" type activities that challenge them intellectually, e.g., pipeline analysis, design and planning. Field technicians work more with their hands (e.g., installation of the plans) and are usually more interested in work that allows them to solve problems and challenges by using their "hands-on" talents. Field operations personnel may prefer more demanding work that requires them to put their "heart" into it.

Unfortunately, many clients I coach are in careers that they fell into by accident or careers that were chosen for them. For example, perhaps your parents always wanted you to become a doctor, lawyer, engineer, or manager, and you wanted to do something else like work as a mechanic or teacher. It is important to become aware of how certain activities make you feel when you're engaged with them. By doing so, you will gain greater clarity around what characteristics your ideal career should include. More about this in the next section on generating and sustaining energy.

INSIDE INSIGHT

The Case of the Clean Sweep

Several years ago while working with a team responsible for keeping the facilities clean in a conservation-related organization, an employee, "Paula" (not her real name), and I were discussing how she became a groundskeeper for the organization. She seemed very bright with the capability to do much more than empty trash cans and sweep the ground. Paula informed me that her parents were quite wealthy with a successful business.

Initially, Paula had pursued a pre-determined path in business to appease them. However, she couldn't see herself chained indoors all day. She enjoyed working outdoors, had a work ethic second to none, derived satisfaction from helping people, and firmly believed in the mission of the nonprofit organization she worked for. She wanted to do her own thing despite pressure to follow in her parents' footsteps.

Paula's parents threatened to withhold financial support if she didn't comply with their vision for her to have a higher status career. However, they hadn't realized the strength of her convictions to pursue her own career independent of what they wanted for her. Rather than surrender to their expectations she swept aside their judgments and chose the groundskeeper position. While she made a career choice that some people would consider beneath them, she was ultimately happier for sticking to her own preferences and the job factors that motivated her rather than giving in to her parents' vision of a successful career.

How would you have responded to this situation? Have you experienced a similar situation?

UNDERLYING NEEDS

We all have underlying needs for security, survival, belonging, love, growth, etc. The activities we engage in provide us with avenues for getting these needs met. If you are finding yourself in the wrong career, perhaps you have been "under the influence" of others.

It's like letting someone else drive your car. If you have a strong need to either "please others" or "keep the peace," then you may end up compromising what is important to you, or accommodating others more than you should. There is nothing wrong with those needs but they can become problematic when they are influenced by others rather than self-determined. As mentioned at the beginning of this chapter, preferences are those things that you would do *without* the influence or expectations of others.

As human beings, we have other needs as well. The importance of such needs vary by individual. For example, they may include having a degree of challenge and purpose, balance between work and personal demands, financial security, freedom to control your work, having a sense of empowerment, structure and organization, a preferred pace, continuous learning, ability to make an impact, and having fun just to name a few. When these needs are met, we feel fulfillment and show up as our best selves. When unmet, we carry negative emotions and are likely to act out in ways that are unhealthy, childlike, or toxic.

The magic is to identify a career that matches your core underlying needs. There are probably several career options available that allow for your needs to be satisfied, even the needs for pleasing others and keeping the peace. While there is room in most jobs to please others or keep the peace, some examples of careers that offer significant opportunities to please others are commonly found within service-oriented industries or occupations. Examples are customer service representatives, administrative assistants, salespersons, restaurant servers, hotel concierges, and flight attendants. Careers that lend themselves to having someone who needs to keep the peace include negotiators, mediators, security personnel, police, and child social workers.

GENERATING AND SUSTAINING ENERGY

Energy is one of the invisible elements in the pipeline model, but its benefits are perhaps the most tangible and enable us to get the most from our daily lives. Without energy, you probably have little or no "life force" or motivation. Your life feels static and you feel stuck. With energy, you feel alive and intrinsically motivated to interact with the world around you.

You have a certain amount of energy that you either generate or obtain, convert, and expend daily, just as an energy company does. Like a natural gas company, this energy cycle is a product of taking a natural resource and converting it into something you can use to power your everyday life at work, home, and community.

There are several *types* of energy (e.g., gas, electric, solar, geothermal, wind, hydro-electric, biogas, etc.). There are also different *sources* and *availability* of energy (e.g., shale deposits, sun, wind, decomposition of organic material, animal flatulence, resources such as coal, wood, corn, etc.). Each source of energy has different *properties*. Some are more powerful, some are cleaner, some are more stable and reliable, and some are longer-lasting. Some *types* of energy are more sustainable or longer-lasting than others.

ENERGIZED   EXHAUSTED

How does this relate to you and your career? The career equivalent of energy is motivation. Knowing what energizes you and de-energizes you can dramatically increase your satisfaction, performance, and success at work. Likewise, knowing the type of energy you thrive on, how you generate it or where you get it from (sources), what opportunities are available to access it (availability), and how long it keeps you going (properties) are clues about the types of activities, situations, and environments that should be part of your career blueprint, as discussed in Chapter 5, *Chart Your Purpose*.

Identifying the sources and types of energy that enable you to bring your best self to work are often revealed in your preferences as discussed earlier. That is, there is a set of activities, situations, and environments that tend to energize or de-energize you when you are immersed and engaged in them.

Those activities, situations, and environments that energize you are typically things that you either consciously or unconsciously seek out. You are naturally drawn to them because they are pleasurable to you, and you are likely to voluntarily engage in them. For example, you may be energized by creating new programs, analyzing complex problems, helping someone in need, streamlining a process, spending time on a hobby, or talking with others. As a result of spending more time on sources of energy, you will practice them more, and when you practice more, you typically get better at them—assuming that you learn from mistakes along the way and develop good habits.

Conversely, there are also activities, situations, and environments that "de-energize" you and leave you exhausted. These are typically activities, situations, and environments that tend to create a great deal of stress for you. Therefore, you will naturally procrastinate or avoid them. Examples may include confronting a difficult person, making a presentation, writing a report, analyzing data, negotiating a purchase, or commuting to work.

INSIDE INSIGHT

God Bless Diversity!

Immediately following a company restructure my department was split in two and a new boss, "Matthew" (not his real name), was appointed to lead our group in Los Angeles. At his first meeting Matthew complimented us on the various talents we had on the team and expressed a desire to leverage them. He asked each of us to go around the table and share with the rest of the group which types of work we love to do and hate to do. Basically, he wanted to know which things energized us and which things de-energized us.

When it was my turn, I shared with the group the activities that I really enjoyed and the ones that sucked the life out of me. I said that I absolutely hated doing expense reports, scheduling meetings, and "administrivia." The common element among my de-energizers was the super-detailed activities that I was capable of doing, but tended to procrastinate or avoid.

As we went around the table, one of my colleagues volunteered that she loved being the "go-to" person for all the small "get-it-done" type tasks. When I heard this, I couldn't help but blurt out, "God bless diversity!" You see, the very things that I detested doing were the very things that my colleague derived a great deal of satisfaction from doing.

How might you partner with coworkers to increase your energizers and reduce time spent on the things that de-energize you?

Energizers and de-energizers are very individual. In fact, the very thing that de-energizes your coworker, friend, or family member may energize you. Knowing this, being clear on what works and doesn't work for *you* becomes critical versus adhering to the advice of someone else's view of what you should do.

This is not to say that there's a "perfect" job waiting for you out there containing 100 percent energizers and zero percent de-energizers. Even the *best* jobs have at least one or two undesirable attributes that may de-energize you. What I am saying is that being clear about your preferences will enable you to re-align your current position or choose your next position more wisely—greatly tipping the odds in your favor and increasing your satisfaction.

Questions to consider:

- What preferences do you have? If you had your own way, what would you choose?
- What are the underlying needs at the root of your preferences?
- What ideas, activities, situations, and environments energize you most? What do you naturally gravitate toward?
- What exhausts you? What are you de-energized or de-motivated by and naturally avoid?
- How do your personal preferences and motivators match with the business needs of your job or company?
- What underlying needs and energizers are being satisfied in your current job or career? Where are you dissatisfied?
- How might you create some win-win situation with coworkers so that you are working more from areas of strength and career preferences?

To know what you prefer instead of humbly saying Amen to what the world tells you you ought to prefer, is to have kept your soul alive.

- Robert Louis Stevenson,
Scottish novelist and poet

UNEARTH YOUR
PRINCIPLES AND VALUES

Character is like a tree and reputation its
shadow. The shadow is what we think
it is and the tree is the real thing.

- Abraham Lincoln, Sixteenth U.S.
President who abolished slavery

What do you stand for? The beliefs you hold
and attitudes that you carry with you each
day speak volumes about what is important to
you. They are indicators of the core principles and
values that you live by.

One of the core operating principles in the natural gas industry is to ensure the safe and reliable transmission, storage, and distribution of gas for customers. Natural gas is a highly sought-after product that offers enormous benefits to consumers. In line with that, one of the core values that many companies have is being of service to others and being a dependable community partner.

For instance, when decisions are made about what pipes to purchase, the engineers and supply management professionals (buyers) will typically err on the side of purchasing pipes that can withstand a higher standard of pressure than required by law. Why? Because the values these experts hold dear include quality, maintaining integrity of the system, and providing reliable and safe service to customers. By leveraging the inherent values that exist in the pipeline as well as the people who operate the pipeline, gas companies are able to adapt to changing needs while providing valuable energy that, in turn, can provide light and warmth to millions of people.

Likewise, our personal principles and values help guide us to a sense of higher purpose and fulfillment. In essence, principles are beliefs or standards while values reflect the underlying meaning or importance attached to such beliefs or standards. When you operate in alignment with your core principles and values you are able to operate with integrity and wholeness. In a sense, your principles and values serve in ways similar to valves that open and close to regulate the flow of gas through a pipeline. In this instance however, they regulate the amount of passion that you are able to express and put to use at work.

Values include such notions as integrity, knowledge, collaboration, fun, excellence, adventure, financial security, family, and accomplishment. Why are they important? Your choices affect your quality of life. For example, let's say that one of your core values is "strong close knit family relationships." Imagine that you just got the "perfect job" that will allow you to provide adequately for your family, yet the job comes with a three hour round-trip commute each day. This is three hours of time added to your regular work day that severely restricts "family time." Will the tradeoff be worth it to you in the long run?

Often our values are invisible to us, yet they drive a significant amount of our actions. For example, let's revisit the value of close-knit family relationships. This value spills over to your work "family" as well, and it is certain to be activated when your work team is experiencing conflict. Your natural reaction may be to restore the team to a place of harmony, whether it is by softening positions and attempting to mediate the dispute, or by reaching out and trying to smooth things over.

Alternatively, you may avoid the team conflict situation altogether until it blows over if that has been your default or preferred coping mechanism. If you value being competitive, being the best above the rest, your natural reaction during the team conflict may be to assert yourself and directly challenge others and stir up conflict.

Effective adaptation to pressures in your work environment can be a smart and productive means to get things done and achieve results. Similar to how operators proactively or reactively adapt to changing operational, environmental and customer pressures, you also adapt throughout your career on a regular basis, either proactively or reactively. These adaptations may be sparked by external pressures (e.g., family, friends, coworkers, or bosses.

There is a tipping point to adaptations that becomes detrimental to your personal and career health. Stress and dissatisfaction normally intensify as you stray further and further away from your core principles and values. Whether you realize it or not, pushing on without conscious awareness of your core values robs you of the key asset of your overall health and vitality. This can manifest as a liability in the form of lower productivity and work quality, increased relationship challenges, and chronic health issues.

Understanding who you are and what you stand for is crucial for mastering yourself and your career. Knowing your true self can serve as your ally in re-focusing when life's demands pull you off balance. When your work is aligned and congruent with your principles and values, you can achieve uninterrupted fulfillment or "flow."[6]

This alignment typically reaps greater satisfaction and leads to optimal performance and better health. As a result, you will be less likely to feel compelled to compromise what is most important to you. When your principles and primary values are at odds with your daily work activities and environment for a significant period of time, you are likely to stray from the true essence of who you are and what you stand for.

This congruency extends to your unique personality and that is the subject of the next chapter.

---

[6] Flow is similar to being "in the zone." Essentially, it's a relaxed state of mind where you are also deeply focused and engaged in what you're doing. A typical outcome is peak performance and sustained energy.

Questions to consider:

- What are your principles and values? What attitudes do you have toward work and life?
- How do they match up with your current job? Are they aligned? If not, what is incongruent?
- What do you believe and value so strongly that it would be difficult to give up, even at the risk of being penalized in some way for how you go about your work?
- What beliefs, if any, may be holding you back from achieving your goals and fulfilling your dreams?

I had chosen to use my work as a reflection of my values.

- Sidney Poitier, Oscar-winning actor, film director and author

CHAPTER 9

EXPRESS YOUR PERSONALITY

What lies behind us and what lies before us, are small matters compared to what lies within us.

- Ralph Waldo Emerson, American essayist, lecturer and poet

Bringing who you are to what you do each day helps define, in part, the unique contribution you make to your organization and to those you serve. It is how you "show up" and behave at work.

Natural gas has certain attributes that show up in a unique way. These attributes affect how the gas performs and how people experience and interact with it. Its properties include lacking smell or taste, being stable, invisible, lighter than air, versatile in how it can be used, and storable for long periods of time without losing its potential.

Natural gas behavior changes in rather predictable ways when extreme pressure is applied in the pipeline. In fact, pressure beyond the pipeline's capacity can be an invitation for a deadly explosion. Furthermore, natural gas properties can be altered under different temperatures. For instance, natural gas turns into a liquid when it is super-cooled. When warmed back up, the molecules expand and turn back into a gas. The default state is gas form. Yet, while natural gas may change form, the basic molecular structure is still the same. Such attributes of natural gas enable us to identify it and to work with it in beneficial ways.

Similarly, you have certain attributes that are stable over time and identify who you are, and they reflect how people experience and interact with you. You have certain attributes and you behave in unique ways just as gas does. We call these personalities! Different attributes of your personality typically intensify or lessen under different conditions.

Personalities are as varied as the types of jobs there are. Some personalities lend themselves better to certain jobs. Just as it is instrumental to ensure your values and skills are a match for a particular job, a satisfying job includes one where your personality is a good fit, as well.

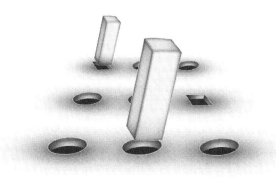

Each job has innate characteristics that call for individuals to behave in certain ways in order to perform those jobs successfully. You have preferred ways of interacting with others that reflect your personality. A job that involves engineering expertise and quality control typically requires someone who is calm, methodical, detail-oriented, and conscientious. If you have a boisterous personality with a fast-paced work style, you could be like a bonfire next to a leaky gas pipeline. Conversely, if the position involves introducing a product or service to new customers, someone with a boisterous personality and fast pace may be a more suitable fit. That position is likely to require the ability to reach out and build rapport with prospective customers quickly and influence decision-makers to buy your product or service.

Likewise, finding a good fit with your personality and the company, department, or team culture is equally important. For instance, if you are an extroverted, visionary "mover and shaker" who thrives on change and you are working on a team of low-key engineers, you may become frustrated by the slow pace of decision-making and lack of stimulating conversation. To place you on a team of energetic, hard-charging account executives is likely a better match. The bottom line is that your personality offers key indicators about how well you match with the inherent demands of a particular career.

INSIDE INSIGHT

Who are You?

When freely expressing your personality you bring *"who you are"* to whatever job you do. What follows are some questions that can point to your personality make-up.

- At the end of a long day, do you decompress and recharge by spending time alone on the couch watching television, reading a book, running, or daydreaming? Or do you prefer socializing with a group of people at a local bar, restaurant, party, or group activity?

- Are you naturally more intuitive, future-oriented and able to see different possibilities, or are you more inclined to draw upon precedent and past experience with a preference for tangible, in the moment, hands-on focus?

- Are you one to make decisions with your gut (subjectively) or do you rely more on making decisions with your head (objectively)?

- Do you crave order and sticking to a plan or are you more comfortable simply having a general direction while keeping your options open?

- Do you tend to be more trusting, expressive, and optimistic or more skeptical, reserved, and cautious when building relationships with others?

- Are you direct and "to the point" or informative and "suggestive" in your communications with others?

- Do you tend to initiate communications or respond to requests from others?

- Do you prefer to influence others through data and logic or through emotional and relationship appeals?

- Do you prefer routine and stability or variety and change?
- What kind of pace do you prefer?
- How do you behave under pressure?

How might knowing more about yourself and your personality affect your career choices?

In the pipeline business it is common to use a chemical additive called Mercaptan, which alters the natural state of gas from a scentless substance to one with a distinct odor. This is done for safety reasons so people can more quickly detect a leak. Similarly, the chances are that you adapt or modify your natural style to fit the demands of your work and surrounding environment. Adapting to different circumstances is necessary and advantageous in order to get things done. Whether it is healthy for you depends on how much you need to adapt on a regular basis and how much stress it creates for you.

Conversely, there may be times when you fail to adapt, or even fail to notice the need to do so, and you stay in your comfort zone. In turn, this can make you less effective. However, having a clear and accurate perception of your personality is important for determining whether or not a particular job or work environment is a good fit for the long run.

Being able to express yourself clearly and truly while bringing your best personality traits to your work is your unique contribution to the job and the company that employs you. How people experience you at work also contributes to your reputation and perceived potential.

The degree to which you express your personality at work will also be reflected in your overall performance. This is the focus of the next chapter, *Monitor Your Performance*.

Questions to consider:

- How do you characterize your personality? How do others describe you?
- What type of work and work environment are the best fit for your personality?
- Under what conditions do you thrive and perform your best? (E.g., low, moderate, or high stress conditions?)
- How do you behave when pressure and stress rise and fall?

At the very least, looking on the bright side offers a better view.

- Eliza Rhodes, Writer and philosopher, author of *Sign Language*

CHAPTER 10

MONITOR YOUR PERFORMANCE

There are no traffic jams on the extra mile.

- Zig Ziglar, Author and motivational speaker

As far as career advancement opportunities go, demonstrating strong and steady performance is your "ticket to play." To understand why, let's examine what happens in a pipeline system. The consistently strong performance of a section of pipe instills confidence among various stakeholders (e.g., procurers, engineers, and operators) because it can be counted on to carry out the job of distributing gas safely and reliably.

Engineers test and verify a pipe's performance under varying conditions. Passing such tests provides a competitive edge to pipe suppliers. From a procurement perspective only those materials that meet stringent qualifications are approved for purchase and deployment in the field. Field personnel who install and replace pipes sign off on completed jobs. Otherwise, inferior pipe materials may slip through and thereby lower the quality standard while potentially increasing safety risks. Solid performers are commonly viewed by others as consistently delivering results. We will first discuss the importance of "getting results" for your career and then subsequently delve into the "ART" of performance, Attitude, Relationships, and Talent. These are the three factors that my "stuck" clients consistently overlook when evaluating their own performance.

GETTING RESULTS

A pipeline system is constantly monitored, assessed, and evaluated for how well it is performing. When there is a significant deviation or decline in performance, system operators determine if intervention is required. A pipeline system that fails tests or has excessive corrosion merits attention to determine the cause. It must be monitored closely and frequently until it performs consistently so operators and customers can trust it.

As with a pipeline system, having a consistent, strong track record of your performance is an entrance condition to being considered for advancement by most leaders. Therefore, having a way to monitor, evaluate and measure your performance is equally important. Typically, you need to demonstrate steady and acceptable performance over time to be competitive for new opportunities that arise.

There are occasions when you may struggle with assigned tasks and projects. One of the gravest mistakes I see employees make is not asking for help or not asking for help early enough when they are struggling with a task or project. Meanwhile, the deadline for completion looms near and they are silently suffering because they are afraid to ask for help, or they do so when it is practically too late to do anything about it. I call these folks "Silent Stewies" because they are needlessly and silently stewing with angst.

Have you ever silently hoped things would magically work out? There is often an implicit fear that you will look incompetent or weak if you ask your peers or boss for help. However, how incompetent will you look once the deadline passes and you either have low quality output or none at all? At this point your boss has very little room to explore alternatives.

Additionally, your boss is likely to lose face with peers or superiors when your team is unable to deliver on a commitment. Bosses don't like surprises. A better option is to seek assistance earlier to get the clarification or support you need while there is still plenty of time and there are potential options available.

Here's the bigger picture. The risk of not asking for help soon enough is that it will ultimately reflect poorly on your performance. If this becomes a pattern over time, it will affect your standing with your boss, team, and organization. Your reputation may become a "Last Minute Mary" or "Incompetent Charlie."

If you let your performance slide over time to the extent that you are put on a performance improvement plan it is important to be clear about the root cause of your under-performance and how to fix it. Otherwise, expecting a promotion or new assignment in light of poor performance is likely to be a fruitless endeavor. As a poor or mediocre performer you are going to have a limited audience who will listen to you and consider what you have to say. Strong performers will find it much easier to gain the attention and support of others for attaining their career goals.

While your past performance often provides a key indicator about your capabilities it is certainly not the only one. Perhaps you are in an inhospitable work environment, a narrowly-defined job, or you haven't been given the opportunity to develop some hidden talents and showcase what else you can do. If you feel you are miscast in your current role, or typecast in a job that does not play to your interests and strengths, it is imperative to clearly communicate your situation to your supervisor or a trusted advisor as early as possible.

By informing others *before* there is a chronic performance issue, or erroneous assumptions begin to solidify about what your capabilities are, you retain a more realistic chance of seeking out and securing opportunities that nurture, cultivate, and showcase your hidden talents. For example, you may have public speaking ability, artistic skills, or project management strengths. Regardless of how your career conversation with your boss goes, the key is to show up, perform to the best of your ability, and bring who you are along with your talents to each job you find yourself in—even when the fit is not quite right.

Traditional views of performance tend to focus squarely on results, the outcome of your actions. In reality, performance is multi-dimensional. I encourage you to look at performance as more of an ART form as introduced at the beginning of this chapter.

The interplay between having a positive Attitude, strong Relationships, and diverse Talents enable high performance in an increasingly interconnected and interdependent workplace.

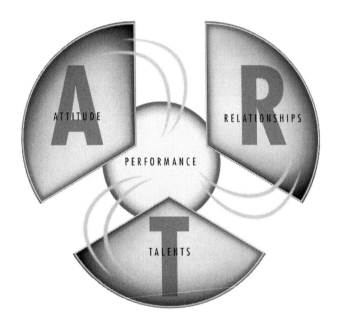

ATTITUDE IS PART OF PERFORMANCE

Your attitude is a vital dimension of your performance. Your attitude can either amplify or exacerbate the impact of how you relate to others and your overall effectiveness at work. How you "show up" at work is critical to success, yet this variable is frequently overlooked. Bringing *who* you are illuminates your character for all to see. What I mean by *"who you are"* is your authentic and best self—it is internal to the fabric of your being. *"How you are"* you are refers to how you show up at work which is more externally-based—it is how others experience and perceive you at work day-to-day and in stressful situations. Bringing *how* you are can create a positive or negative impression among those around you.

Allowing yourself to have a negative attitude can seal off the pipeline before you have a chance to explore potential options. Being closed-minded or pessimistic or cynical limits your potential in two ways. First, it cuts you off from seeing viable possibilities that are right in front of you. Second, it makes people wonder how flexible and adaptable you are.

People who are closed-minded are more likely to place blame on external sources for their lack of career advancement and fulfillment, whereas those who are most successful know the secret is to be open-minded and receptive to feedback.

INSIDE INSIGHT

The Case of the Broken Fences

Once I was facilitating a succession planning meeting with a leadership team of Directors who were brainstorming about candidates for a Director level position. The name of a particular project manager, "Marty" (not his real name), came up as a candidate. While Marty's boss was extolling his virtues and describing Marty as a great performer a couple of other Directors were flinching.

When Marty's boss was finished one of the other Directors turned to Marty's boss and the rest of the group and told a different version of Marty. This Director shared that his employees continually came to him frustrated about Marty's behavior on projects that they needed to work on together. The nature of their complaints was about Marty not being a team player, that Marty cared only about himself, that he was uncooperative and bullied the others to get his way on things, he regularly failed to respond in a timely manner after repeated requests for information, and he took credit for accomplishments that were not entirely his.

During further discussion, another Director told about a similar experience when working with Marty several years previously. All this information about Marty's "other side" was news to Marty's boss. He hadn't realized that as charming and respectful as Marty was with leadership, he stepped all over his peers and left a trail of hurt feelings and soured relationships among co-workers he encountered along the way. Subsequently, the Directors in that meeting determined that Marty needed to be coached by his boss about the need to change his behavior and mend fences with his peers before he could be seriously considered a viable candidate for a Director position.

What role do you think attitude and relationships play in your overall view of someone's performance and potential?

It is natural to become disenchanted and frustrated when you're in a situation that is not fulfilling or meeting your expectations. Be aware that if left unguarded, such emotions can negatively affect your attitude, skew your thoughts and actions, and turn off those individuals who can help you. A pessimistic attitude is likely to attract dead ends. Cynical attitudes are like pipeline shut-off valves that stop the flow of potential career opportunities.

On the other hand, optimistic attitudes fuel "what if" thinking and open valves; allowing possibilities to flow more freely. Therefore, it's important to keep a positive attitude. Having a "can-do" spirit is infectious and generates greater possibilities and enthusiasm that others pick up on.

Be what you want to attract! Optimistic thinking may not attract everything you desire (I'm not encouraging Pollyanna thinking), but at the very least it sends subtle signals to yourself and others. By making the most of your current job and performing at a satisfactory level, you are more likely to bring your dreams to fruition.

RELATIONSHIPS AS PERFORMANCE ENHANCERS

A second dimension of performance that my clients often overlook is the ability to build and maintain trusting relationships with others. Employees and leaders who have developed positive and strong relations with others stand out in a positive way when being considered for new opportunities.

A common client question or complaint I have heard over the years is about a client questioning the legitimacy of a decision that has been made regarding the promotion of a peer, or assignment to a highly desirable project team. The justification is almost always the same—that the employee is more competent than their peer. In these circumstances, what is important to note is that there are relationship factors that decision-makers value just as much, if not more than, technical ability.

For example, if you can draw upon strong trusting relationships with individuals from other departments, you can usually get things done with a quick phone call that otherwise might take a team many months using normal procedures and communication channels. Conversely, decision-makers will shy away from providing you high-profile opportunities or bringing you on board if you have a track record of poor relationships. If you think mostly about yourself while disregarding the needs and concerns of others, you are essentially creating roadblocks to future career opportunities.

TALENT WINS THE BENEFIT OF THE DOUBT

It's a given that we are going to slip up every now and then. Even for the most talented among us, we all have days when we make a big mistake or we are not able to bring our "A" game. The extent to which you focus on and contribute your natural talents at work, the better your overall performance will be in the long run. The better your track record of performance and your abilities, the greater benefit of the doubt you are likely to receive when not performing at your best.

In the pipeline business, there are thousands of things that must go right in order to ensure a smooth operation. Occasionally, whether it is pipeline failure or human error, there are times when a company makes a mistake that ends up as an item on the evening news. Customers and the public at large are more likely to give a company the benefit of the doubt when they have a stellar reputation and track record. Occasional mistakes get treated like anomalies.

Likewise, managers will tend to give you a greater benefit of the doubt based on your typical level of performance. Your manager may be more inclined to overlook your mistakes or shortcomings when you have a track record of solid performance versus an inconsistent and less trustworthy track record. Take time to reflect on this and evaluate yourself as if you want to hire someone like you.

Questions to consider:

- Do you perform consistently and reliably? Would your boss agree?
- What natural talents do you have that you can use in your current role?
- In what areas do you struggle and need to ask others for help?
- How would others on your team characterize your ART skills (attitude, relationships, and talents)?
- Based on your track record, to what extent have you earned the "benefit of the doubt" from others?

> *An ounce of performance is worth pounds of promises.*
>
> - Mae West, American actress, singer and playwright

CHAPTER 11

UNCOVER YOUR BLIND SPOTS

Your mind is like a parachute.
It only works when it's open.

- Anthony J. D'Angelo, Author
of *The College Blue Book*

As Pogo Possum, a comic strip character, once said, "We have met the enemy and he is us." One of the biggest obstacles that you'll likely encounter along the way to achieving your career goals is the most challenging to see, yet it is hidden in plain sight. It's you. It is crucial to increase self-awareness, including your beliefs and behaviors that may be holding you back from getting where you want to go.

We all have blind spots and areas to improve. Sometimes we need to get out of our own way. If we are not aware of our blind spots they become obstacles to our success and become a source of ongoing mystery and frustration about why we're stuck. Some people have strengths that are not fully exercised at work due to lack of opportunity or awareness.

Many people fear negative feedback and view it as an unwelcome, painful experience. It takes a lot of courage to own both the positive and negative aspects of ourselves. Some say "ignorance is bliss." In the case of your career, ignorance may be a career killer and therefore can dramatically affect overall career potential.

Safety is a primary area of focus within a gas utility organization. This includes safety of the field personnel who are dispatched to different locations each day, as well as the safety of customers. Drivers are taught techniques that are designed to increase their awareness of their surroundings. One of these techniques is to perform a "circle of safety" before getting into their vehicle and backing up or driving off to their next job. Drivers who unfailingly walk completely around their vehicles prevent potential accidents and injuries.

The reason is obvious when you think of toddlers playing. Some toddlers who park themselves behind trucks have been saved by diligent drivers who walked around their entire vehicle before getting in it. Even with all the mirrors there are still blind spots. Only one life saved by taking precautions makes the extra effort worthwhile.

We all have blind spots too. Have you discovered any blind spots in your career? Increasing your awareness of your surroundings is essential to uncovering blind spots. You can get yourself into trouble when you lack awareness of your environment.

People who dig into a pipeline with their home equipment such as a shovel or a rototiller learn this the hard way. At best, there may be a gash in the pipeline which emergency crews can fix before anyone gets hurt. At worst, a spark created by the tool's impact can ignite the gas and result in a deadly fire or explosion. With the pipes below the surface at various depths, customers are blind to what is underneath until it is too late!

There is good reason for people being advised, to call 811 before digging, the underground utilities service alert phone number in the U.S. Field personnel armed with detailed maps or blueprints can mark the locations of underground pipes, and customers can avoid dangerous maneuvers.

Likewise, we all have blind spots in our careers. Common career blind spots include being unaware of our strengths, weaknesses, and the perceptions and expectations of others. In fact, we are considerably blind to some of our strengths because they come so naturally to us and we take them for granted. We erroneously assume that others are just as capable of our strengths as we are. In a sense, our talents are hidden from us. Still, for career success, we need to increase our awareness of our talents to be able to seize opportunities and capitalize on them.

On the other end of the blind spot spectrum, many employees who talk with me are frustrated about not advancing in the company as they do not understand *why* they are not advancing.

INSIDE INSIGHT

The Case of the Righteous Ranting Man

I have seen many clients who have the best intentions, but simply are unaware of how they come across to others. One such client, "Randy" (not his real name), is a bright and vocal member of a team that I was working with on a consulting basis to help the team work more effectively. He came to me one day incredibly frustrated with the way he was being treated by his boss. He said, "Mike, I'm the one who says what everyone else is thinking, but they are too afraid to say it. I get reamed by my boss and my peers when I speak up and state the obvious."

The way Randy described the situation it sounded as if he was getting punished for sticking his neck out in front of the team. We agreed that I would sit in on an upcoming team meeting and observe how the group interacts. At the meeting the team was seated around a large conference table. They were working on a solution to a problem they had been experiencing. At one point during the rather lively debate Randy stood up, slammed the palm of his hand on the table with a thunderous cracking noise, interrupted the person talking, and shouted, "That's a dumb idea! We should…." His boss immediately chastised him and told him to sit down.

After watching the reactions of both his team members and his boss I got plenty of clues about what was holding back Randy's career. After the meeting when Randy and I debriefed what happened, he said, "See what I mean, Mike? I spoke up and then my boss reamed me. He says he wants a 'safe to say' work environment, but he really doesn't want different opinions."

Technically, Randy was right. He did speak up with an unpopular opinion and he did get flak for it from his boss. However, Randy failed to be aware of or acknowledge *how* he spoke up. To him, it was a normal way of expressing himself. To others it was intimidating and disrespectful.

If you were advising Randy, what suggestions would you have for him to handle such situations more effectively in the future?

While many companies still promote front-line supervisors and team leads with decisions heavily based on technical performance, there is actually increasing focus on relationship-building skills as you go higher in organization leadership.

Employees clamor for promotions or other choice assignments and then complain when they do not get them. However, some employees fail to notice they are underperforming in their current jobs.

Someone who is gifted at building relationships but struggles with producing actual results is going to be viewed as an underperforming employee, as well. These employees are sometimes said to be "all smiles and no substance."

Despite what your aspirations may be and how clearly you seem to be qualified, you may have blind spots holding you back. Others may perceive that you are missing a piece or two that is necessary for a particular opportunity. Therefore, more than you realize, your capabilities to succeed in certain roles may be limited.

Do you need to perform well in all aspects of your job? Not necessarily.

When I review the results of career assessments with clients and we look over their strengths and weaknesses I advise them to put any feedback they receive into the proper context for the type of job or career they are considering. It may be possible to find a way to manage around certain weaknesses.

For example, one of the lowest-rated competencies my clients usually receive feedback on is related to financial acumen. Is that a development need that you need to focus your improvement efforts on? It depends on what your current job involves, as well as where you want to go in your career.

Let's take a deeper dive. If you are a software developer and your passion is to spend your day programming computer code, then financial acumen may not have much relevance. Relevance comes into play when comparing and evaluating financial acumen with other competencies that you could be working on, such as communication and collaboration with coworkers and customers. However, if you have ambitions to move into a manager-level role where you will be responsible for budgets and possibly profit and loss responsibilities, increasing your financial acumen skills takes on much more relevance.

Honestly evaluate how your strengths match with the core competencies of the career you want. If the areas you are weaker in will not play a significant role in where you want to go, it becomes a moot point to focus on that. An alternative to consider for maximizing your performance is to focus a greater amount of your attention and energy on your strengths rather than your weaknesses. In fact, a best practice is to leverage your strengths and identify ways to manage around your weaknesses.

Understanding three key ingredients that are fundamental to cultivating your potential will help you better position yourself in the eyes of others for future opportunities. This is the focus of the next chapter, *Understand your Potential*.

Questions to consider:

- Do you suspect that you may have some blind spots?
- How much time do you spend reflecting on your talents and strengths?
- Who can you ask for feedback about potential blind spots that are holding you back?

> *The greatest of faults is to be conscious of none.*
>
> - Thomas Carlyle, Scottish essayist, satirist and historian

CHAPTER 12

UNDERSTAND YOUR POTENTIAL

As human beings, our greatness lies not so much in being able to remake the world...as in being able to remake ourselves.

- Mahatma Ghandi, Leader of the Indian Independence Movement

As you develop and mature from childhood to adulthood you grow and adapt in response to your environment and the circumstances you encounter along the way. In the process of becoming mature you discovered new things you could do that you had not done before. Through practice and persistence, you probably became more skilled at some of these. This is similar to the pipeline business.

While the core method of delivering natural gas to customers via a system of pipes has remained virtually unchanged over the past one hundred years, the natural gas business is constantly changing. There are continually new pipeline-related technologies being introduced, increasing regulatory requirements and policies, changing customer needs, and fluctuating availability of natural gas that affects prices.

The life expectancy of a newly installed pipe can be up to one-hundred years. A pipe's potential lifespan depends on its quality, maintenance, and upkeep over the years. It's the same with your lifespan! Pipes wear out over time and either need to be repaired or replaced at some point. Similarly, how well you tend to your own upkeep over time can positively or negatively impact your lifespan.

Your career isn't much different from the pipeline containing energy that flows through it. The pipeline has its own potential "lifetime expectancy" for delivering gas before its ultimate demise. Your career has its own lifetime expectancy as well, and it also depends on how well you take care of it. Not only is your career dependent on how well you take care of your personal pipes, but it also is affected by where you get and cultivate your own sources of energy for powering your potential contributions and accomplishments.

The determination of when a pipe needs to be replaced rather than repaired or upgraded often depends on how well it performs during pressure testing, (as discussed in the previous chapter, *Monitor Your Performance*). In a pipeline system, having equal pressure in front of and behind the gas will make it stagnant. Without pressure from behind, or demand "downstream" from customers, the gas will remain stagnant and not move. A combination of increased pressure and demand creates movement.

You probably have also had times in your career when you felt stagnant. What happened to your personal motivation? For whatever reasons you realized that you can contribute at a higher level than your stagnant position. Increasing a healthy amount of pressure at work can create the necessary motivation and movement to advance your career.

Having a strong, compelling and clear vision for your career (as discussed in Chapter 4, *Chart Your Purpose*), and understanding what you are most passionate about (as discussed in Chapter 5, *Discover Your Passion*), can combine with your willingness to take on constructive challenges that push you out of your comfort zone to create a positive force that draws you forward. You can break free from career stagnation.

You may have times in your career when you have plenty of motivation but feel like you are reaching the limits of your capacity to contribute to the team and your company. In the natural gas industry, a company can reduce its risk of becoming obsolete by upgrading smaller pipes with larger, higher capacity pipes. The notion of upgrading pipes applies to your career as well.

You may need to upgrade your career potential by learning new skills, techniques, or knowledge that expand your capabilities in order to meet the current or future needs and demand in your workplace. During your career there are also times when your services are in greater demand than at other times. There's a natural ebb and flow.

Alternatively, do you have hidden talents that your team and company would benefit from, but you don't share them, possibly because of a lack of motivation or opportunity? Like pipes that are well-maintained and have excess capacity beyond what the company may need at any given time, you may believe that you have untapped capacity. That is, you have more to offer than what you are being asked or tasked to do.

Through a regular review of a company's pipelines an engineering analysis may determine that a pipe is being used beneath its potential capacity.

The extent to which a pipeline's excess capacity for carrying additional gas has value to the marketplace from a supply and demand point of view, company marketers can reach out to large users of natural gas and inform them that they can take advantage of the extra capacity that is available. In effect, the company learns to leverage the asset to increase revenue and further benefit the organization, customers, and shareholders.

This principle works for you and your career as well. The extent to which you proactively develop your knowledge and skills, the greater is your capacity and ability to provide additional value when called upon by your organization. Your value to your team and organization increases immeasurably when you are positioned to address future needs that they may need to draw upon.

A premium exists in the minds of prospective natural gas customers to the extent that the company operating the pipeline is reputable and has a positive track record. Brokers in the natural gas industry want suppliers who can be counted on to deliver the needed product in a timely, safe, and reliable manner. Similarly, leaders notice and assign a higher premium or value to employees with good reputations and positive track records. They want employees who not only can perform today but also possess the capacity to meet the business needs of tomorrow.

Fortunately, people are more dynamic than pipes and natural gas. If you are not continually growing and changing with the times, your value to your team or company is likely to diminish and you risk becoming as obsolete as a corroded pipe with leaks in it. If you fail to maintain and take care of yourself over time, you may wear out (or burn out) and reach the limits of your capacity.

Ultimately, you also have a lifespan within any career and company you work for. How long your career lasts, and in what capacity, is strongly linked to both your perceived and demonstrated track record and potential.

THREE A's OF CAREER POTENTIAL

Career potential encompasses a blend of three facets that are integrated into a common whole: aptitude, aspiration, and attitude. During a company's talent review and succession planning process[7] a few of the main questions leaders ask when considering someone's potential for a promotion or lateral move are:

---

[7]The talent review process is one by which leaders will discuss and evaluate an employee's key strengths, development needs, and the next steps needed to enhance his/her overall value and attractiveness for potential opportunities in the organization. The succession planning process typically goes hand-in-hand with talent reviews. In developing succession plans, leaders identify a pools of employees who can step in and fill specific positions should the incumbent be promoted, rotated, or leave the organization at some point in the future.

- Does this employee have the ability or aptitude to successfully perform the job or group of similar jobs?
- Does this employee desire or aspire to do a job like this?
- Does this employee demonstrate a positive attitude? That is, is the employee enthusiastic, thoroughly engaged and committed to contributing to the company's success?

If the answer to any of these three questions is "no" or "not sure" when *you* are being discussed it isn't necessarily a dead end for you, but you will certainly need to find ways to more positively position yourself in the minds of leaders making such decisions.

3 A's OF CAREER POTENTIAL

Let's take a moment to delve deeper into the "Three A's" of potential.

The first is *Aptitude*. In the pipeline business, a pipe's specifications provide operators with a rough idea about whether or not the pipe has the basic capability for the task. For example, specifications include the thickness of the pipe walls, how much stress the pipe walls can withstand, and the diameter from one end of the pipe to the other. These specifications inform operators about the pipe's capability.

When leaders are sitting around a table discussing potential candidates for various positions, they want to know if you have the "essential specs" that would enable you to succeed in a future assignment or a specific position under discussion. They are looking to determine if you have a solid foundation to build on and fall back on if you take on a challenging assignment or new position.

With regard to your career potential, your leaders want to consider the various conditions and degree of pressure situations that you have successfully navigated. In the pipeline business, operators will "test the lines" to make sure everything is in working order before officially putting the lines into operation at full capacity. It makes perfect sense, right? Carrying a greater load could mean greater benefits to the organization and its customers, but it could also mean greater danger and disaster should things go wrong.

It is in everyone's best interest that pipelines are tested at different levels and conditions. Therefore, in considering you for a new position that is different from what you are currently doing, or is even a few steps beyond, they will likely consider whether you performed similar tasks successfully at a lower level. However, your aptitude is just one aspect of your potential that leaders discuss and evaluate.

A second dimension of potential is *Aspiration*. What good is it for leaders to consider you for a potential manager position if you have little to no desire to be a manager or to lead others at some level? Knowing this, it becomes a waste of time to discuss you as a candidate for a particular position when it is known that you have no desire to move up or move to a different work location where the opportunity may be situated.

It is important to position yourself for future opportunities by clarifying and communicating your career aspirations with your boss and others where you work. As a facilitator of these talent review and succession planning meetings, I'm continually amazed by how many leaders in the room do not know their employees' career goals! Granted, many individuals being discussed are often two to three levels below where top leaders are within the organizational hierarchy. Aside from the responsibility of leaders to be in touch with their employees, it is also wise for you to make sure that your boss and your boss' boss are aware of your career goals.

Consider a lesson from the pipeline business. Sometimes pipeline operators will "oversize" a pipeline system. By using pipes larger than the current need, they are anticipating *future* needs and *growth* possibilities. Identifying and communicating your personal career aspirations get results like a pipeline system that is designed with future growth in mind. You will be positioning yourself for consideration for future possibilities beyond the scope of what you are doing today. This positioning can influence and stoke people's imagination to see you in a different light and think about what it will be like to have you in a role that you aspire to have one day.

Unlike individual pipes where capacity for growth is essentially defined the moment they are manufactured with certain specifications, you differ in that you can learn, grow, and influence how your capabilities are utilized throughout your career. Therefore, it is time to initiate a career conversation with your boss if you haven't already done so.

It is equally important to keep your boss and others updated about your aspirations as your situation changes so they are operating with *current* information whenever they conduct talent review and succession planning discussions. You don't want your boss operating under the assumption that you are not interested in a particular type of career opportunity based on a conversation you had with him or her a few years ago when your personal circumstances and career goals were different. For example, if the reason you are not interested in a management position is that you want to be home with your kids until they start kindergarten, then it's important to let folks know when your situation changes and you have more flexibility and desire to take on a different position.

Clients often ask me if they will be blacklisted for turning down an opportunity that is offered to them. My answer is generally, "No." It usually depends on how you handle it. There may be a number of reasons why you might turn something down. For example, it may not be of interest to you, you may have young children at home and you want to keep the flexibility you have now, you may be caring for an elderly parent and are unable to move farther away, you may be in school and lack the bandwidth to take on new or greater responsibility, or perhaps you are in the middle of a challenging project that you feel obligated to finish before considering new opportunities. Those are all legitimate reasons to turn down an offered opportunity. You can minimize potential negative repercussions for the future as long as you demonstrate gratitude for being extended the offer, and provide a reasonable explanation as to why this is not the right fit or the right time for you.

A third dimension of employee potential is *Attitude* (which is also one of the dimensions in the ART of Performance). Would you hire someone on your team who is constantly complaining, critical of others, short on solutions, putting in minimal effort, is focused on his/her own interests at the expense of the team's interests—and generally has a negative attitude and brings negative energy into a room, as well? Well, neither will your company's leaders! Don't be that employee.

What leaders often look for in selecting an employee is whether a person has potential and if they have a positive "can-do" attitude and if they go the extra mile to get a job done when needed. Nobody shines brighter than an employee who sees a problem or challenge and takes the initiative to propose a solution and tackle it. Or an employee who accepts an unpleasant task that no one else wants without complaining and makes the most out of it. Leaders want to be assured that any employee who is being considered for a stretch opportunity is engaged and "committed to the cause."

Sizing up employee potential is often a matter of trust. First, leaders need to trust that you have the basic ability and capacity to successfully perform the job under consideration. Second, they need to trust that the opportunity aligns with your personal goals.

Lastly, they need to trust that you will be a positive role model for others and give it your all.

What helps you build your potential? Just as there are means available to extend and increase the asset value of pipelines, there are also many strategies you can use to maintain and increase your value and overall potential within your company, no matter how long you've been around!

The next chapter discusses important strategies for increasing your potential value and desirability as a *human* asset within your organization: building your personal brand, networking and relationship-building, and ongoing professional development.

Questions to consider:

- Are you clear about what you want?
- Who is aware of your aspirations? Who should be?
- What excess capacity do you have that would benefit your company?
- What are you doing to prepare for tomorrow's opportunities?

With realization of one's own potential
and self-confidence in one's ability,
one can build a better world.

- Dalai Lama, Tibetan
spiritual leader

CHAPTER 13

BUILD YOUR POTENTIAL

*Successful and unsuccessful
people do not vary greatly in
their abilities. They vary in their
desires to reach their potential.*

- John C. Maxwell, Author
and motivational speaker
on leadership

Building your personal "brand" is an essential,
yet often overlooked dimension of career
potential. It involves your personal image,

reputation and the extent to which you live up to it in the minds of leaders, peers, direct reports, customers, and others. The culmination of consistently demonstrating your aptitude through solid performance and initiative, clearly communicating your focus and aspirations, and demonstrating a positive attitude through various conditions creates your strong reputation among others in the company, and outside the company, as well. Your reputation—good, bad, or indifferent—is similar to what may come to mind for you when you think about a familiar company or product.

Brands are all around us. What images, emotions, and thoughts do you have when you hear Apple, Google, Coca Cola, Zappos, Target, or Toyota? Your reaction may be based on first-hand experience with one of their products, or through word-of-mouth from friends, family and acquaintances, online reviews, third party awards and reviews, etc. In any case, your degree of familiarity with a company and positive or negative association with them most likely plays a significant role when you make daily purchasing decisions. Just as companies have brands, you do too! In fact, you have a brand whether you realize it or not!

INSIDE INSIGHT

Validating Your Brand

Companies recognize the value of having a strong brand and will often try to use it to differentiate themselves from competitors. There are independent companies that measure and report this. The consumer polling organization, J.D. Power, and the consumer product-testing organization, Consumer Reports, are well-known among industries and consumers alike for their various awards such as the highly coveted "#1 in Customer Satisfaction" and "Best Overall Value" awards and for the stamps of approval they confer on worthy organizations in a wide array of industries and products and services.

Such awards help build trust and enhance a company's reputation among prospective consumers who otherwise might not be familiar with a given company or product. In the energy utility industry, a favorable reputation can make real differences with state and federal regulatory agencies, municipal governments, public media, customers, and neighborhoods in which the utilities operate.

Additionally, websites such as yelp.com and glassdoor.com provide open forums for customers and employees to comment on their personal experience with a company's product or service. Likewise, glassdoor.com enables current and former employees to share insights with prospective employees about their experience working for a particular company. Reviews on these websites often influence buying decisions that prospective consumers depend on whether or not the reviews present a company, product or service favorably or unfavorably.

What about your personal brand? How can you determine how well it measures up to who you are and who you want to be?

As we discussed in the earlier chapter, *Uncover Your Blind Spots*, there may be significant gaps between how you view yourself and how others experience and perceive you. Do you know what instantly comes to mind among peers, direct reports, customers, and leaders when your name comes up in conversations? Leaders make decisions in part based on how familiar they are with you and if there is a positive or negative association in their minds. How people experience you affects your image and reputation, your personal brand. Therefore, awareness and active management of your personal reputation or brand is essential.

In fact, companies that recognize the value of strong brands go to great lengths to protect them. For example, marketing and communications personnel at a pipeline company take extra steps to ensure the accuracy of maps that they must provide to fire departments in each neighborhood where they provide service. Fire departments need to know where all the pipelines are located in the event of an emergency. Therefore, the mapping department is wise to ensure that the proper and up-to-date maps are sent with properly affixed company logos to minimize confusion among firefighters when responding to an emergency situation.

In building your potential it is helpful to have a sense of who notices you and who you know that can help you. Just as a broad network of pipes helps ensure the stability, performance, and capability for dealing with unforeseen circumstances in delivering natural gas, the breadth and depth of your personal network helps others in your company become familiar with you and get a sense of your aptitude, aspirations, and attitude.

One of the most common mistakes I see employees make is adopting a mindset of letting their performance "speak for itself." What many employees don't realize is that this singular reliance on performance is not enough. Many high performing employees keep to themselves and remain quiet about their accomplishments. Unfortunately, in talent review and succession planning discussions, many people in the room routinely have limited or zero first-hand knowledge about who they are, what their career goals are, and what they are capable of contributing to the company. If you don't want this to be you, don't get discouraged. The good news is that you can change what people know about you!

There are several ways to change your brand. Before you do anything else, get clear about what you want your brand to be compared to what your brand actually is today. Start by acknowledging your brand (even if you only begrudgingly accept it) and then identify steps to shape it in the desired direction. There are a few essential ingredients to changing your brand.

1. Visibly and significantly change your behavior and performance so that it is consistent with the brand or reputation that you want.
2. Develop strong relationships (and mend broken ones) with people who can advocate on your behalf.
3. Increase the size of your network so that more parts of the organization become visible to you and you become more visible to them.
4. Continue to develop your skills and abilities.

Establishing a broad network enables you to develop meaningful relationships with a cross-section of individuals at different levels of the organization who can help you be more effective in your current job, provide you with an avenue to learn about potential career opportunities that may be a good fit for you, and potentially advocate on your behalf.

Are you demonstrating your capacity and growing as a professional? Optimizing the value of a key pipeline involves sizing up how much marginal capacity is available beyond what is needed by the company to serve the core needs of its customers. Similarly, employees who contribute discretionary effort beyond what is needed or expected will stand out from peers as having greater potential. As we noted earlier, leaders take notice of employees who take initiative and step forward for tackling projects and problems, who volunteers their efforts for initiatives that help the organization as a whole, and who continually strive to improve themselves.

Many of my clients have been raised in cultures that discourage "standing out" from the crowd. For them, the emphasis has been on uniformity, cooperation, and deference to authority. The wisdom of "the nail that sticks out gets hammered down" is an old saying that comes to mind. While being a good team player is essential, remaining invisible and blending in with everyone else is likely doing you a disservice when it comes to advancing your career.

I'm not encouraging you to be narcissistic and pound your chest about how great you are. However, I am advocating that you find ways to make your contributions, unique talents, and career aspirations known to others in your organization.

The analogy I made at the beginning of this book about being an actor in your career fits here. As uncomfortable as it might be for you to be "on stage," it is essential to go there sometimes—even if it's backstage—rather than simply blending in with the audience. When it comes to your career and personal brand, every interaction you have, or don't have, can make a difference in shaping a decision-maker's impression of you and what you can do.

Meanwhile, there are probably talents that you have not used in your current role because the:

- Job doesn't call for it.
- You don't think it's valued.
- There are others on your team who fill that need.
- You don't derive satisfaction from exercising it.
- You have a blind spot and don't recognize your talent as such.
- Your company or team culture suppresses it.

Sometimes you may perform beneath your true potential due to lack of self-confidence or perhaps the influence of your surrounding environment. Untapped potential is a lost opportunity not only for you, but for the company you work for. Regardless of the reason, there are often opportunities to showcase your talent elsewhere in the organization or by volunteering in the community. Have you ever had someone who believed in you, recognized and pointed out talents that you never even considered, and mentored you? Letting others see you exercise such talents can shift their calculation of your overall potential and create new opportunities that were previously inaccessible to you.

Some ways you can increase your potential are by continually developing your strengths through taking stretch assignments, attending workshops, taking temporary jobs, mentoring others, getting involved with cross-functional committees, taking online and peer learning opportunities, or hiring a career coach to help you focus on what you want and to enhance your skills. A key to effectively building your potential is to use multiple methods rather than rely on any single strategy.

One final thought on potential involves how you respond to stress. Do you break down, blow up or burn up when in highly stressful or heated situations? As in the previous discussion on pressure (Chapter 12, *Understand Your Potential*), stress can be a positive or negative force in your career.

With too much pressure, gas poses a danger to a pipeline system and to people who are in harm's way. When under extreme pressure a gas-filled pipe can rupture. When near high heat, a leaky gas-filled pipe can catch fire or explode. Employees who appropriately respond to pressure and learn to adapt in healthy and productive ways can bolster their personal brand and overall potential.

Do you get too complacent in your job when there is not much pressure? With too little pressure, gas won't move efficiently through a pipeline and its natural benefits will not be completely derived. In the absence of experiencing sufficient challenges, you may be physically present at work, but your potential may lie dormant and remain static. It's often perseverance in difficult and challenging situations that will win over others and have them "singing your praises." This amounts to having a team of enthusiastic fans who will advocate favorably for you and champion your cause when you are not around. This carries a lot of weight among decision-makers.

Your potential is a natural outcome of being in touch with your strengths and exercising your natural talents. Your personal brand is what sells you and connects others to what you care about most. An element that enables you to cultivate and grow both your potential and your brand is "space." Having adequate space allows you to fill it with options and possibilities. Space is the focus of the next chapter.

Questions to consider:

- What is your personal brand? Do you know what reactions people have about you when they hear your name?
- What do you want people to think, feel, and say about you?
- What do you take for granted that others compliment you on?
- What does your network look like?
- What are you doing to expand your network and increase your visibility?
- What natural talents do you have that you can use in your current role?
- What are you doing to stay current and to freshen or refresh your skills?
- In what ways is your potential shrinking or expanding?

We can easily forgive a child who is afraid of the dark. The real tragedy of life is when men are afraid of the light.

- Author Unknown

MIND THE
SPACE BETWEEN

The only way of discovering the limits
of the possible is to venture a little
way past them into the impossible.

- Arthur C. Clarke, British science
fiction writer and inventor

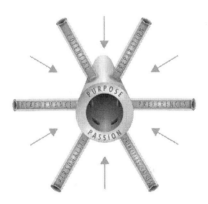

Let's take a look at the role space plays within a pipeline system and how it can apply to your career. Having adequate space plays an important role with the ability to expand your capacity to handle a variety of situations and opportunities as they arise.

One dimension of space is the role it plays *inside* each pipe. As mentioned in an earlier chapter, the volume of gas that flows through a pipe is largely determined by both the size of the pipe and the internal pressure. A larger pipe offers the benefit of being able to transport more gas to customers and safely handle the higher pressure needed to do so. Likewise, the more space you have available offers greater capacity for career growth opportunities and for handling the increased demands of managing your career. Let's face it, life is filled with plenty of daily activities while your mind is filled with continuous thoughts and distractions. It is helpful to be able to clear your thoughts and free up space in your mind. This allows you to relax more and improve your focus while thinking more clearly and creatively.

Having adequate space around the outside of pipes ensures safe operation and can help avoid accidents and damage. Often space between pipes and other structures is needed to account for vibrations that can occur, particularly during an earthquake or from nearby construction. In addition, if there are water lines nearby and they are too close to the gas lines, damage to the gas pipes can occur. For example, field personnel working on a water line may accidently strike a too-close gas line, the coating on a water pipe may cause corrosion with a gas pipe, or water leaking from a broken water pipe may get into a gas line.

As it relates to your career, adequate space between your personal pipelines can buffer you from unplanned incidents as well and maximize your periods of rest and recovery. For example, a client calls you to change a project deadline that is two weeks away but everything is now needed by the end of the week. Knowing what you are capable of doing, and setting healthy boundaries for managing your projects, enables you to deliver what your boss, clients, and others expect without too much disruption.

Another dimension of space is the notion of having a strategic reserve. Gas companies often store gas as part of a "rainy day" reserve in the event of an unexpected spike in consumer demand (e.g., for heating during a cold winter snap) or spike in market prices where quick supplies of energy are needed.

Having such a reserve has multiple benefits. The first is to have the capacity for challenges that arise so consumers will have what they need at reasonable rates. This provides peace of mind for both the company and the consumer. A second benefit is that the company is in a great position to take advantage of opportunities that arise to sell excess gas to other regions of the country at a premium, thus benefitting the company's bottom line and its shareholders, and keeping its own customer rates low. A third benefit is the reputation and goodwill that is created when the company is forward-thinking, reliable, and looking out for its customers' best interests rather than only its own.

Similarly, it is advantageous for you to have your own "strategic reserve" of energy to draw upon as situations arise, e.g., a fantastic new project that will enhance your career development. If you are fighting fires all the time, your capacity to take advantage of new opportunities that present themselves will be limited. Moreover, you will be a candidate for burnout and less likely to perform your best without having periods of rest and recovery. Taking care of yourself is an instrumental element in bringing your best self to work, enlarging your capacity, and advancing toward your dreams.

INSIDE INSIGHT

Catching a Breath of Fresh Air

There was a period in my life, in the not too distant past, when I was scheduled so tightly with client meetings and commitments that I barely had time to catch my breath. I found myself running around day after day to catch the train from San Diego or Orange County to work in Los Angeles (for East Coast readers, this is the equivalent of commuting to NYC from Boston or Providence, respectively). I knew down to the minute what time I needed to leave the office in order to catch the subway and subsequent connection to the commuter train at Los Angeles' Union Station.

There was a certain adrenaline kick I would get every time I was able to squeeze in another fifteen minutes of sleep, or another client meeting, and then successfully dart off to catch the train. This went on for several years. One day a mentor of mine noticed how sick and stressed I was. He asked me how I wanted to experience my life at work. After sharing with him that I wanted to have a meaningful impact with a sense of control and calm, he challenged me about the "train gymnastics" regimen that I put myself through each week.

We got on the topic of energy, as in how much energy I had available to me and how I wanted to spend it. It became quite clear to me in that moment that "catching the train" wasn't necessarily the wisest means of getting my adrenaline rush. What I realized is that just because I *could* catch the train in fifteen minutes door-to-door, it didn't mean that I *should*. It wasn't serving me or my vision for my life.

Where are you misdirecting energy and what opportunities do you have to redirect it?

Adding space inside your mind and between your activities is like adding room to breathe. Just as gas mixes with air to create energy as part of the typical combustion process, space (and fresh air for your brain) facilitate your personal combustion capacity.

Space creates room for possibilities, and revisiting and re-examining old dreams, and exploring areas that you have not moved into yet. As in the example above, having space around you offers opportunities to move into the space and create. Dancers and artists intuitively know this. If you don't have space, you become limited in how you can express yourself. With ample space surrounding you, you'll have greater freedom to try something new.

Space gives you room to explore new territory and experiment with new ideas. It often involves new thinking and courage in order to step beyond artificial boundaries that you have set for yourself, or allowed others to set for you. Space provides you with opportunities to discover new talents or new ways to use your known talents.

When you get too caught up in the "doing" of your workday, your awareness of various career possibilities naturally contracts. Space can allow room for dreams and possibilities that you can examine and play around with. Just as regulators and industry professionals have standards of spacing in and around pipes, meditators have long realized the benefits of focusing on and expanding the *space between thoughts*. Meditation relaxes the mind, increases awareness, restores energy, unblocks constrictions, releases toxins, enhances creativity, sharpens focus, and decreases stress among other health benefits.

A quiet mind and the stillness that ensues from focusing on the space between your thoughts will enable you to reach inward and get in better touch with your true self. By paying attention and reducing the volume of the white noise of your thoughts in your life, you are likely to be better at discovering and figuring out the higher purpose that has always been within you and you can then listen closely to what it is telling you.

Imagine yourself looking in a mirror. The image looking back at you is distorted because you have filters that alter your self-perception. However, when you are in a mindful state without all the distractions, it is like removing distortions from your reflection and allowing you to see what others see. Your true purpose reveals itself in that space and enables you to more closely examine your true nature without distortion.

In addition to removing distortions to get a clear picture of your true nature, it is equally important to recognize and minimize variables that interfere with your core purpose (as discussed in *Chart your Purpose*). Just as having a strategic reserve with adequate space, or capacity, in your mind and schedule allow room for you to invite new opportunities, adequate space *within* each pipe in the system operates in a similar manner.

To move gas through a pipe, operators will increase the pressure behind the gas. If there is too much pressure in the pipe and nowhere for the gas to expand, it may cause the pipe to burst. For the gas to move through the pipeline, it needs to have room in front of it to move into. So, with less pressure in the front end, the gas moves along the pipe and expands into the space ahead of it.

Similarly, when you are under too much pressure with nowhere to release it, you put your health at risk and you may burst. However, when you have space around you and room to breathe, you can move forward as well. You can move into new possibilities. As you've probably experienced at some point in your life or career, you can encounter resistance of some sort, either from yourself or brought about by others. The next chapter will focus on resistance that you can encounter as you build your career.

Questions to consider:

- What kind of space currently exists in your life?
- Are you in need of a strategic reserve? If so, what could you do with the gift of space?
- How will you channel and maintain your reserve and benefit those around you?

We are expressions of our energy.

- Valencia Porter, MD, MPH, Integrative holistic health physician

PART III

MANAGING YOUR CAREER JOURNEY

NAVIGATING RESISTANCE TO YOUR CAREER CONSTRUCTION

Don't let what you cannot do interfere with what you can do.

- John Wooden, Famed UCLA basketball coach

Your career doesn't happen in a vacuum. Change is often messy. Things don't always go as planned no matter how much research and preparation you put into getting a new job, or promotion, or transitioning to a new career. Change is regularly filled with both moments of clarity and confidence mixed with moments of confusion and self-doubt, particularly as the process drags out longer than anticipated or budgeted. A career or personal change often becomes messy in the same way that about midway through a home remodeling project there are construction materials strewn about. To help you navigate along the way, I'm going to tell you about TLC for your career.

Project managers are mindful of three areas when embarking on a pipeline construction project to anticipate, address and alleviate potential resistance. I refer to this as the TLC approach. This approach considers the *timing* of the project, the landscape or habitat that will be directly and indirectly impacted by the work being done, and the *connections* and care with which the company responds to a community's particular concerns.

As it applies to your career, TLC essentially entails addressing *external* resistance and obstacles you may face. The when, where, and who of your career construction are about when to make the change, where you want to go or end up, and who else will be impacted by your change.

TLC APPROACH

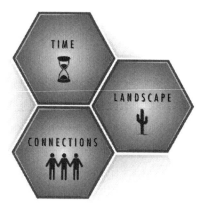

Let's take a look at how natural gas companies navigate resistance that they typically encounter as they're building or extending their pipelines.

TIMING

It is important to decide if the timing is right for a project because of seasonal weather patterns, neighborhood support, economic conditions, endangered wildlife, day or evening shifts, other infrastructure changes going on at the same time, and more. For example, in the case of a natural gas company expanding its pipeline system into new areas, or replacing existing pipes, one of the typical considerations is the timing of such changes between nesting seasons for endangered species of birds. This is called a known obstacle, or constraint. I'm sure you've faced your own share of known obstacles as well!

By anticipating this obstacle and having experience navigating around it, pipeline project managers and construction crews are able to work around nesting season with relative ease and minimize additional cost to the company and its customers. An upside to this is that the company can generate goodwill in the affected communities by supporting efforts to protect endangered species and their habitats. Knowing what is important to impacted stakeholders during times of change can facilitate achievement of mutual objectives. In this case, there is a triple win. The welfare of the birds likely to be impacted, the community that possess a love of nature and value themselves as stewards, and the pipeline operators who want to be good stewards as well and complete the project in a timely and cost-effective manner to serve the company's customers.

It's important to note that the same timing approach will not work for everyone. Each community is different and has different timing needs.

Seasonal Factors

For example, I know of a business community in an upscale, quaint coastal neighborhood that voted to have their main street ripped up and have all pipeline installations put in at once over a compressed six-month period in order to "get it over with." This was different from a historically significant community that voted to allow a redevelopment project to be "spread out" over time and completed in phases.

Likewise, understanding the concerns of your "neighborhood" of family, coworkers, bosses, clients, and anyone reporting up to you may be just as important when examining timing of any career changes you are planning. In fact, there are several timing-related considerations to factor into your career construction plans.

For example, your boss or coworkers are likely to think about how much of your work they will need to absorb if you move on. One effective strategy you can utilize, particularly if you're working on a major project, is to wait for completion or reaching a natural milestone before you move on. This goes for family considerations as well. A typical timing-related issue my clients have faced involves waiting until their youngest child reaches kindergarten or completes elementary, middle, or high school. Likewise, you may intuitively understand that trying to make a job or career change when you are overcommitted, ill, or caring for a newborn or an aging parent can be a very stressful time.

And just as pipeline operators do not use a "one size fits all" approach, you need to craft a career construction plan that takes into account your specific needs and circumstances.

Time of Day

Because of the additional noise from the operation of heavy machinery and vehicles that accompanies most construction projects, residents frequently voice concerns about when construction can take place during the day. For example, city inspectors and city planners may require pipeline construction personnel to stop all work between the hours of 2:00 p.m. and 4:00 p.m. each day which may go against the most efficient way to do business.

Understanding the concerns that are most important to a neighborhood and identifying ways to reduce impacts or offset those concerns with something positive can go a long way in heading off unnecessary resistance and getting needed support.

The time of day is an important consideration in your day-to-day pursuit of career opportunities. For example, many employees structure their job search by conducting search activities and interviews in the early morning, lunchtime or after work so as not to disrupt performance and other people, or mix personal business with work.

Pace and Duration

Going at a slower pace will allow you to maintain other important aspects of your life like a personal exercise regimen and social activities. A faster pace might entail temporarily sacrificing those things until you reach a goal or secure a new position. Just as there are alternative strategies in a pipeline construction project in the face of obstacles, you can develop alternatives for your own career construction project.

You can facilitate your career transition by planning ahead to reprioritize or renegotiate your commitments. For example, your partner may need to carry an extra load for a period of time to enable you to have the opportunity to pursue job leads or go back to school. Or perhaps you need to take a part-time job to ease the financial pressure and emotional strain of caring for a newborn or aging parent.

- What timing issues do you need to consider?
- What adjustments to your plans can you make?
- What pace of your career change will be the most manageable?

LANDSCAPE

Sometimes the solution isn't a timing issue. With a pipeline project it is important to consider *where* a gas company lays its pipes. There may be environmental threats to precious historical sites. There may be sensitive habitats and wildlife in the vicinity of the proposed pipelines that fall under regulatory protection. Likewise, people who live in the affected areas may have economic or safety concerns about such matters as the supply of gas, proximity to a water system, aesthetics, and safety and health of nearby residents and employees. Moreover, residents may fear that the pipelines will have a negative impact on their property values. Concerns such as these can escalate fear and resistance within a community.

For your career it may be important to consider where an opportunity is located, as well. Differences in pay, neighborhood, or quality of living may be important factors for you. A project manager position in one department or city may be a better fit for you than in another department or city.

Having a keen sense of the landscape is a crucial factor for avoiding and offsetting potential harm and the resistance a company may encounter no matter how desperately needed a gas supply may be. As such, flexibility is typically required to negotiate solutions that will work for everyone involved. In effect, what often happens is a company will make detours that were not in the original construction plans. Likewise, you will need flexibility to make detours that were not in your original career plans.

Other forms of resistance include neighborhoods that don't want disruptions such as streets being torn up. These people are often referred to as "NIMBYs," an acronym for "Not In My Backyard." These are individuals or groups of citizens in residential or commercial areas who oppose changes or interruptions in their vicinity that they believe pose a danger to their way of life. Planners need to be able to draw up alternatives. In fact, pipes may need to be routed to go sideways, down the hill, and back up another hill to get to the intended destination. Some routes are less desired than others due to construction costs, potential hazards, safety, and ongoing maintenance concerns. Therefore, pipes cannot always be laid in a direct line to transmit gas from one location to another. Often, they need to be rerouted to go around sensitive habitats and unsafe environments. In addition, during negotiations a gas company may agree to purchase, set aside and preserve a significant plot of land as a way to obtain necessary "right-of-way" permissions and to offset any harm their project may cause.

Similarly, things will rarely go as planned in your personal career construction. You'll experience various setbacks along the way. When embarking on any career change, there are likely to be a few naysayer voices who don't agree with the direction you want to take. Some naysayers may even be your own internal voices. For example, perhaps you finally got offered your dream job, but your significant other threatened to divorce you if you moved the family in order to take it. Ultimately, you need to decide how much weight to attach to any voices and decide about the personal tradeoffs you are willing to make in order to pursue your dream.

In addition, here are some additional setback scenarios that you may identify with:

- The economy tanked and your company had to lay you off.
- You took a lower-level job to get your foot in the door at your dream company, but discovered that the work environment was toxic and not what you thought it would be.
- Your boss told you that you were being groomed to eventually take his or her position only to discover that one of your peers ultimately got the job.
- You finally clicked with a fun-loving group of coworkers who "work hard, play hard" only to get a strict new boss who embraces the philosophy of "work hard, work harder"—and with fewer resources.
- You just read a company email announcement stating that there has been a reorganization that will result in you and your job being transferred to another team that is yet to be determined.
- You went back to school to get a degree to improve your marketability for future job opportunities, but realized halfway into it that the pressures of working full-time, taking care of your family, and going to school were too much to handle.

INSIDE INSIGHT

The Door behind the Detour

Recently a friend and colleague, "Jake" (not his real name), had an interesting journey come full circle. He was young, ambitious, married with a young child, and burdened with a large amount of student debt hanging over his head. His career goal was to get a promotion and make more money to help him pay off his student loans and buy a house.

Several years ago, he left his company in San Diego for a promotional opportunity at an investment banking firm that was across the country on the east coast. His wife resisted, but they moved anyway. Not only did the job come with a promotion and more pay, but it also enabled his wife and him to purchase a home and be closer to their families. Shortly after arriving, he realized that not only was the work environment incredibly demanding and stressful, but the daily three-hour roundtrip commute from the new home was grueling and didn't allow him much time to spend with his wife and child. He realized it was not the quality of life that he wanted.

He and his wife decided they wanted to move back to San Diego, which had felt like home to them. Unfortunately, he wasn't able to find a job there. He then uprooted his family and moved two more times over a three-year period (while also having a second child). However, he remained both optimistic and persistent about achieving his goal to eventually end up in San Diego again.

When I asked him if it was worth all the moves he indicated that each experience was valuable and ultimately helped him realize what was truly important to him. Although he makes less money now than before, he ended up with a great organization, has only a ten-minute commute to work, and has a lot more family time. He still has heavy student loan debts, but they don't seem to weigh on him in the same way they used to.

When have you taken unexpected detours to achieve a goal that was important to you?

How well you deal with various setbacks is important. The most persistent and creative problem-solvers succeed the most often. Just as a pipeline project may be full of detours, you may need to make some of your own detours to reach the career destination you want.

Your career change or transformation does not occur in a vacuum. Therefore, it is important to consider where your plans may impact not only yourself, but also your immediate environment, and consider potential ripple effects that your career construction will have on others around you. You may encounter resistance from your environment and pressure to keep the status quo.

- What environmental conditions do you need to keep in mind as you plan your career route?
- Are some routes safer or riskier than others? Do some routes create a greater chance of leaks or accelerated wear?
- What detours have you made in your career?
- What is the best, fastest, or most optimal way to your career advancement if you can't get there in a straight line from here?
- What detours may be necessary in the future to enable you to achieve your career goals?

CONNECTIONS

When a utility needs to expand in new areas it quickly becomes aware of all the neighborhoods that a new pipeline construction or retrofit project will impact. Often, city inspectors and permitting agencies will place restrictions on what happens with all the soil and sediment that is dug up in the process. People may support the project in concept, but they do not want their neighborhood or Main Street ripped up for three months while the company's field personnel lay pipe.

Extending or replacing a pipeline often means disruption to people's day-to-day lives and welfare. This can take the form of extra noise, increased difficulty for residents and customers to access their homes and patronize businesses, inability to park, difficulty for family and friends visiting, additional dust and pollutants in the air, lights shining into people's homes late at night, etc. Therefore, it is important for pipeline operators to understand how the company can complete its project with the least amount of disruption to surrounding communities. The same type of forethought and consideration is necessary for how your career construction may impact others around you.

Neighborhood residents, business owners, and even city workers in affected communities often fear and resist implementation of anticipated changes. Sometimes the result is dramatic protests, fiery debate, political posturing at city hall, and costly delays. To that end, a company that is proactive will consider how it might offset or mitigate the impact of its project and perhaps compensate a community for their trouble. The most effective strategy is to engage affected stakeholders in advance, long before the first shovel hits the dirt.

Similarly, it is wise for you to anticipate reactions you may receive as you begin to make your career changes so you can proactively take steps to engage your stakeholders as early as possible.

How a company goes about communicating its pipeline construction project with impacted stakeholders such as residents, businesses, civic leaders, environmental groups, local media, etc. is critical to a successful project. Therefore, conducting an effective construction outreach campaign to establish and maintain relationships with affected community stakeholders is an essential element in achieving the company's goals. One of the biggest mistakes a company can make is not doing sufficient outreach, or not doing it soon enough.

One of the biggest mistakes you can make career-wise is not asking for help early enough. A planned outreach campaign will help you utilize your own network of relationships to aid you in getting where you want to go.

In a pipeline company an outreach campaign involves identifying, listening, and addressing the unique needs of community stakeholders. For example, many pipeline companies have embarked on updating all the existing meters with more advanced technology. The companies that navigate potential community concerns effectively are investing in extensive education and communication efforts including community forums, going door-to-door, conducting media interviews, hanging flyers on doorknobs, etc. Their overarching goal is to optimize pipeline efficiency and performance while mitigating negative impacts or changes on the communities where pipes are being placed. This is a back and forth process of enlisting the buy-in and support of the community.

Just as all the pipes in a natural gas system need to fit and work together, a gas company and the community need to fit and work together. Just as it is important for company planners to identify impacted stakeholders, influencers, and advocates, it is necessary for you to do the same. In a sense, you can think of your task as putting together a "career campaign."

When planning a career or job change, it is important to be mindful of potential ripple effects it may have on others within your ecosystem. Think of yourself as being connected to an intricate system of pipes and networks that generally strives to regulate and protect itself from disturbances and imbalances. To help minimize resistance, you can anticipate and engage your network of coworkers, family, friends and acquaintances in your career journey, all along the way. This effort becomes part of conducting your own community outreach.

Having a strong network is essential. Your network must include people who will advocate for you. While some people in your network may be avid supporters of your newfound purpose and direction, you may find that others may not be so thrilled.

Family and coworkers alike who have grown accustomed to relating to you in a certain way, and counting on you for certain things, may feel your change is a threat to them. For example, team members may be focused on how your prospective change may impact them with an extra workload if you change roles. Other team members may be envious of the attention or treatment you are receiving and perceive it as unfair. Therefore, being in tune with what is at risk for your stakeholders and what they believe they will be losing is needed to inform your approach.

Just as with a pipeline system, a change in one part of the system can affect other parts of the system. For example, if a pipeline has a new construction project next to it with one hundred homes, additional pressure will be needed for the pipeline to supply all the new connection points. Otherwise, it won't be able to adequately supply the new homes with needed gas. Moreover, the pipeline system may need to be upgraded to handle the needed increase in pressure.

Your desire to change may increase the pressure on family and coworkers to change as well. Just as operators of a pipeline network attempt to maintain equilibrium of pressure, people you interact with may try to contain your change efforts in order to keep things the same. Every system tends to reset and restore itself to a new equilibrium, i.e., the system as a whole adjusts to accommodate changes. With persistence to reach your goals and fulfill your vision, you can work with your personal network to establish a new state of equilibrium, as well as establish one that better aligns with your career and life goals.

Just as a company goes about communicating its pipeline construction project with impacted stakeholders, how you go about communicating your career construction project is essential, as well. Like it or not, you need to have the support of your community. Though you may see the value and benefits clearly, others may not. The more allies and vocal supporters who speak on your behalf will increase your chances of getting that opportunity you want. For your personal redevelopment and transformation, the solution may be more in the process you use and how you go about making your desired change.

Perhaps making a few adjustments to your construction plan, (e.g., to your route or timing), while staying true to your passion and purpose and principles and values, will make implementation of your plan much more viable. Consider how you tend to look at and evaluate the obstacles and setbacks that you encounter. Evaluate the changes that are needed. Having a positive frame of mind when faced with challenging situations becomes ever so crucial.

Questions to consider:

- Who are your stakeholders? Who do you need to influence and gain support from (e.g., decision-makers, significant others, etc.)?
- Who else might be impacted by your career change? What will your change mean for coworkers, family members, and others who depend on you?
- What routes will you choose to pursue your new career direction?
- How might you need to adjust the method or means by which you make your goal a reality?

So far we've explored the external considerations when creating a career change. However, the greatest obstacles typically involve *internal* factors. Those are the focus of the next chapter, *About Personal Fear and Taking Risks*.

I cannot do everything, but I can do something. I must not fail to do the something I can do.

- Helen Keller, Author and
advocate for people
with disabilities

ABOUT PERSONAL FEAR
AND TAKING RISKS

Progress always involves risk.
You can't steal second base
and keep your foot on first.

- Robert Quillen, American
journalist and humorist

Just as your external environment can make or break your success, so does your internal environment. In a pipeline environment, a change in one part of the system affects other parts of the system. No change occurs in a vacuum. Each operational change can typically have short and long-term ripple effects. For example, changing the pressure of a pipe in the transmission part of the system (which uses very large, high pressure pipes) can affect the delivery of gas to customers who are part of the distribution system (which uses smaller, lower pressure pipes). There is typically a regulator station in between, and its job is to bring down the pressure to a rate that the smaller pipes can use to deliver gas to people's homes. A shutdown of one part of the system to make necessary repairs often requires adjustments to pressure and valve openings and closings made elsewhere in order to continue the uninterrupted flow of gas to customers.

You are a system too! You have your own "operating system" which strongly influences your ability and capacity to implement changes in your career. The operating system is made up of your body, thoughts, emotions, and spirituality.

Unless you have x-ray vision or other special senses, you must be able to break through the surface to see underneath your personal operating system and understand how your own network of pipes may be contributing to your career situation. For example, many of my clients blame others for their lack of advancement without being clear in their own hearts and minds what they really want and why they want it. In fact, these same clients have passed up terrific development opportunities without acknowledging to themselves that they are too afraid of taking the chance of going after what they want. Secretly, they are hoping for a guarantee that things will work out well if they make a move.

In your own transition, you will find that changes to one part of your life affect other parts of your life, either positively or negatively. A "better" job that involves more stress may affect you physically and mentally. Another job or career that entails addressing employees in conflict on a regular basis may affect you emotionally and spiritually.

RISK-TAKING

Making a career change involves risk. Likewise, operating a natural gas pipeline inherently involves risk. Moreover, any change to the system requires thorough planning and thoughtful deliberation to ensure safety of the system and employees, and to ensure that communities are not foreseeably placed in harm's way. The wrong decision, or careless performance, or neglect can have disastrous consequences. Likewise, doing nothing to address safety issues and "hoping for the best" is rarely an acceptable solution.

Interestingly, many of the clients I coach are often quick to "play it safe." Unlike a pipeline system which presents life and death scenarios, rarely does a career change involve life or death scenarios. However, you may be treating career change as if life or death rules the roost, and as if there aren't ways to handle what comes your way. This is where taking charge of your career involves being courageous.

What my clients (and you, also) may do is undersell your own capacity to handle whatever comes your way. What you may fail to acknowledge is that there are risks, known and unknown, all around you every day. Yet you still make decisions, adapt, and get through each day. Ironically, "playing it safe" and maintaining the status quo usually means you will remain stuck in the very situation you want to change.

Playing it safe and doing nothing is one of the surest career killers. You may tend to be ruled by fear and overemphasize the potential downside of challenging situations. One of the underlying assumptions is that by avoiding change, you will not get hurt. This is simply a fallacy. Rather than remaining paralyzed, arm yourself with as much information as you can about potential risks involved with your career change and thereby empower yourself to deal with them. This will enable you to plan a way for moving forward while minimizing risks. I advise my clients who are feeling stuck to consider establishing a goal of creating a more balanced perspective that emphasizes focusing on the potential benefits while accurately assessing and mitigating risks of change.

When embarking on any new situation, your natural tendency may be to resist change. Interestingly, some people are energized by the prospect of changing jobs, while others are paralyzed with fear by the same prospect. If you fall into the second group, look for clear and realistic information about what the job or career path entails and you will usually rid yourself of much of your anxiety about change.

Sometimes refocusing your attention is a gentler, less abrasive, and more productive use of your energy. By bringing attention back to both your passion and purpose (as discussed in Chapters 4-5) you will find an essential starting point for rebuilding or redesigning your system of pipes. This in turn can ignite the necessary energy to manifest your desires and arrive at your desired destination. This awareness also becomes a key advantage and a lever for sustaining yourself during internal or external resistance and obstacles that you encounter along your career journey.

Sometimes you can be your own worst enemy. The way you have designed your environment (i.e., your personal blueprint) may lead to foreseeable outcomes that adversely affect your efforts to achieve what you want. You may not even realize that the flow of energy in your own system is compromised in some way while it is sabotaging your efforts and holding you back.

OVERCOMING OBSTACLES

We all have setbacks and they may be physical, psychological, or emotional. What separates individuals who succeed from those who do not succeed is persevering and not letting obstacles stop them. Setbacks may slow you down, for sure, but often there are ways around them either through discovery or invention. Successful people take the extra step of anticipating obstacles and risks, and they develop a plan for addressing them when they appear.

INSIDE INSIGHT

The Case of the "Unsupportive" Boss

"Vanessa" and "Maria" (not their real names) worked together on the same team. They felt that their boss was too impersonal and didn't care about their career growth. Vanessa and Maria separately asked me for an individual coaching session about their respective careers. After hearing them I learned they both blamed their boss for holding them back and not getting them opportunities to advance their careers. After inquiring about what would be an ideal career opportunity for each of them, they both struggled to articulate what it was that they wanted. They knew they wanted something new or different. After further exploration and some clarification of what they were passionate about, and the kinds of roles and activities they enjoyed, they both indicated they were afraid to make a change to their "dream jobs" even if those jobs were magically offered to them.

They lacked a clear vision of where they wanted to go and the confidence to go after it. The root of the matter is that they were letting their fears drive the agenda. This lack of clarity became a major obstacle for each of them. Quite simply, it was easier for them to blame their boss, and make her the scapegoat for their lack of advancement, in order to avoid looking at their own contributions to their situations. In reality, their boss cared considerably about their careers and had made ongoing attempts to help them develop and take on new opportunities. However, she eventually became frustrated with their repeated reluctance and resistance to try something new.

*How do your fears hold you back
from getting what you want?*

With any change that you attempt, you are likely to have a degree of uncertainty and doubt among other feelings that come and go during the process. You may experience anger, sadness, depression, and hope, perhaps in a roller coaster fashion. Honor those feelings, acknowledge them, but don't get stuck in them. Remind yourself about the original reason you wanted the change. Hold onto your vision and your purpose, the reasons for pursuing your path.

The greatest challenges my clients describe as getting in the way of movement toward their career goals are time constraints, inadequate education, insufficient work experience in their area of interest, and having an unsupportive boss. While these are all significant, my experience in working with clients is that there is usually more to the story than what appears on the surface.

Many obstacles are in the eye of the beholder, real or imagined. The top two obstacles that I believe my clients face are fear of change and not being crystal clear about what it is they actually want!

While the external, visible barriers that you encounter when going about your career construction pose a challenge (as discussed with TLC in Chapter 15), the internal, invisible or hidden barriers can be just as formidable. Keeping these internal barriers in mind will help you stay true to yourself and enable you to develop effective strategies for navigating common challenges that you are likely to encounter: fear, pain, resistance, and limiting beliefs.

OVERCOMING OBSTACLES

Fear can be immobilizing. It is an odd thing that some people fear failure while other people fear success. You may feel that the very things you have grown comfortable with may put you at risk, for example, daily routine, work hours, responsibilities, friendships with coworkers, competence in what you do, etc. There may be an underlying assumption that you will not be able to handle a situation or a worst-case scenario that aligns with your fears. There is also a common misperception that after making a change your life may be worse than if you simply took the "safe route" and did nothing in the first place.

Your overall attitude and mindset play a powerful role in addressing obstacles and overcoming setbacks. For example, when you adopt a helpless story or a victim mentality you are giving up your personal power and choosing to let yourself be defeated by obstacles, real or imagined. However, when you adopt a more positive mindset, you are likely to view obstacles as temporary setbacks that can be overcome. I've had plenty of clients who have succeeded in spite of having the above hurdles. By taking the time to develop themselves and work through a problematic situation, they eventually found ways to run around or to jump over hurdles in their way.

The discipline of meditation is instructive here. It teaches you to learn to accept and redirect your thoughts rather than resist them. I have learned in my personal meditation practice that it can be quite liberating to simply clarify and voice my intentions, and then let go of them and trust that things will work out. Essentially what you do is put your desires out there, acknowledging that you do not have control over the outcomes, and then consistently focus your energies on what you really want to manifest in your life. In fact, we will look at what to do when things go wrong in your career in the next chapter, *Dealing with Corrosion and Leaks*.

Questions to consider:

- What obstacles do you anticipate?
- To what extent are you readily able to assess and map your own network of pipes (e.g., principles, values, personality, performance, etc.)? What percentage of your "pipes" is below the surface and more difficult to access?
- What limiting beliefs or fears are holding you back from pursuing or achieving your dream job or career?
- What must you give up in order for your desired change to come true?
- How can you re-center yourself when you are noticeably off-track? What strategies do you find most effective?

Everything that doesn't work out leads us closer to what does.

- Eliza Rhodes, Writer and philosopher, author of *Sign Language*

CHAPTER 17

DEALING WITH CORROSION AND LEAKS

Do what you can, with what you have, where you are.

- Theodore Roosevelt,
Twenty-sixth
U.S. President

As with your career, there are always a number of things that can go wrong with any natural gas pipeline system. One of the most common things that threaten the health of a pipeline system is a leak. Pipes age and can corrode over time due to weather and impurities in the gas that flows through them. At early stages these leaks may be scarcely detectible and the system will still run smoothly, but not completely efficiently. However, larger and more numerous leaks may form over time if signs of corrosion are left unattended.

A leaking pipeline can have serious consequences. When you have a lot of pipeline leaks, the immediate area surrounding the pipeline system is put at risk. The gas can escape into the atmosphere and create a hazardous situation by igniting and causing a fire or explosion. It can also radiate toxic energy that can contaminate and harm people.

The notion of toxic energy has parallels in your career as well. Corrosion and leaks are the equivalent of trouble spots you may encounter, or "mistakes" that you may make and accumulate along the way. The way in which you handle such situations can be very telling and reflects upon you in the minds of others. For example, if you made a lapse in judgment regarding a purchase that you made for your office, do you become defensive and deny it when confronted by your boss or peer? Or do you acknowledge your error and apologize?

Employees who own up to their missteps and take personal responsibility and initiative for repairs will stand out much more favorably than those who simply complain and make excuses for not taking corrective actions that are within their control. This amounts to a "victim" mentality that drains the energy of others. It is definitely not a proactive "victor" or "can-do" mentality. Jumping in and appropriately responding instead of denying and avoiding will stand out to decision-makers who are looking for individuals they can trust to exercise good judgment.

Sometimes mistakes or missteps are not immediately and obviously apparent. They can take years to surface. Pipes typically will have a protective coating or "wrap" that guards against corrosion. When someone has been digging below the ground and hits a pipe and disturbs the coating, it can leave the pipe exposed and vulnerable to corrosion and subsequent leaks in the future. The negative impact of the damage may be delayed for years and eventually worsens over time when ignored.

Many of my clients have done the same with how they handle missteps during their careers. For example, some of my clients repeatedly showed up unprepared for meetings while others have consistently gossiped about peers and revealed confidences to others. They don't realize that they created and worsened their own situation by not addressing important matters head-on from the outset, and they may not realize the cause and effect.

- What leaks exist in your career?
- Which ones are self-inflicted?
- How do you respond when you encounter a leak? What adjustments do you make?
- Do you radiate positive or negative energy when leaks are discovered or exposed?
- Would you want to promote, hire, or take a chance on you based on the behavior that others see?

A third cause of potential leaks is when a pipeline system is over-pressurized due to human error. As pressure builds up, the potential for disaster increases exponentially and can disrupt a natural gas system. Sometimes operators will "vent" the pipelines in order to release some amount of pressure to establish a healthier equilibrium and avoid highly damaging and potentially fatal consequences. You may find that you make mistakes under pressure or stress. When you are stressed in your job, you may make more mistakes.

- How well do you perform and behave under pressure and stress?
- What strategies are effective for you when you need to relieve pressure and stress?
- Are you aware of your core needs and the impact your strategies have on others?

DETECTING LEAKS

Operators in the pipeline industry utilize a variety of tools to assist them in proactively checking the integrity of pipes and detecting early-stage corrosion and leaks before they become a problem. One such tool they use is a Pipeline Inspection Gauge (aka a "smart PIG"). It is a robotic device that moves through a pipeline to help operators gauge its structural integrity and overall health.

You also have ways to measure your career health and skills or behaviors that may need strengthening or replacing. For example, there are personal cues and early warning signs to indicate when you are on a path to burnout. Some signs may include significantly increased anxiety, feeling resentful, preoccupation with or avoidance of your daily work, or surprising reactions from others in response to what you say or do. If you're like me, there are times when you notice your "energy draining and your enthusiasm waning." Being aware and mindful of the things that exhaust you can signal when it is time to recalibrate.

Meanwhile, there are also proactive methods for testing how well pipelines can withstand varying degrees of pressure, essentially a "stress test." Operators will perform something called "hydro-testing" where they fill and shoot water through the pipelines with different levels of intensity to see if the pipes can successfully withstand a pre-determined level of pressure that may occur in the event of an emergency situation.

In a way, you also have a known tolerance for effectively handling varying amounts of pressure and stress from your work and life. For your career, do you regularly test or challenge yourself by tolerating situations that wear you down? Different jobs have different stressors and levels of stress.

Being aware of how you handle stress is important for now and for your future. For example, if you are usually in a low-key environment with a predictable workload such as an assembly line, research lab, or an accounting role, becoming a high volume customer service representative with customers screaming at you all day or a stock trader with constant shouting may not be good career moves. While the money may be attractive, you are not designed to withstand the volatility and pressure of that type of job.

There are additional methods for detecting leaks in pipelines. Have you ever smelled an off-putting, distinctive odor in your kitchen or living room? Have you ever heard an unusual sound such as hissing, whistling near a pipe or a gas appliance? Have you ever seen exposed pipes vulnerable to the elements, a damaged connection, dead or dying grass or plants surrounding otherwise lush areas, or dirt or water being blown into the air? These are all indicators of leaking gas that field personnel as well as informed customers use.

To detect leaks and stress affecting the health of your career, there are several methods you can use. You can look or see, listen or hear, and smell or test for vital signs. This is typically accomplished through observation, soliciting and listening to feedback, and first-hand experiences. An example of observation is to pay attention to what emotions come up for you and how others respond to you when you are dealing with a difficult situation (becoming aware just *before* the leak occurs). An example of obtaining feedback would be utilizing an anonymous survey or individual conversations to get opinions of people you respect (becoming aware *after* the leak occurs). An example of testing through first-hand experience is to compare how others are responding to you in the moment or the results you're getting (becoming aware *during* the activity to determine if a leak has surfaced). Any one of them may be sufficient, but if you use all three you increase your chances of detecting a leak, or potential leak, at an earlier stage.

The earlier you detect a leak, the less costly and less effort it takes to fix it and get back on track. The longer it takes to detect, the higher the potential time and energy to get back on track and the greater the risk of something worse happening.

INSIDE INSIGHT

The Case of the Genius Manager

I recall a time when a colleague of mine, "Cal" (not his real name), was experiencing challenges with his team and was concerned about the cohesiveness of the group. After interviewing the team members, several themes emerged. These issues, including one that was related to Cal's leadership style, were creating stress and dissatisfaction in the group. While working with the team to process issues around team trust, one of the things that emerged was the differences in values each team member placed on information shared by Cal.

One lightning rod issue was that employees felt in the dark about what was going on in the company. Cal explained that he would review all the emails he received and then pass on what he thought were the most relevant and useful, thus saving his employees from ever more overflowing email inboxes.

What was particularly enlightening was that some team members appreciated Cal filtering emails for them and sending on the most relevant information. However, others felt he was withholding information. This was a leak of Cal's that was unknowingly corroding team trust. His employees' preference was that he forward all bulletins he received and let them determine what was important or valuable to them. By making himself vulnerable and seeking out feedback, Cal was able to repair the breach relatively quickly.

On the other hand, had he let the status quo prevail it eventually would have created irreparable harm.

If you had a potentially fatal flaw, would you want someone to tell you what it was?

- What senses can you use to detect leaks that may be affecting your career?
- What leaks do others observe? Do they see you as you see yourself? What do

you hear them saying about you and your performance?

- Are there any connections or relationships that are broken and need fixing?
- Just like an exposed pipe, when do you feel exposed or threatened?

FIXING LEAKS

Learning more about your personal system of pipes and the inherent risks enables you to devise a plan to manage leaks, fires, or explosions that divert you from your desired career path. For example, some leaks and explosions that some employees have detonated include angrily pounding on a business meeting room table, cutting corners on safety procedures, continually interrupting coworkers, telling off the boss, and missing major project deadlines without asking for help or providing a heads up to those relying on you.

You may have certain behaviors or habits that corrode your personal brand or performance. Not all "fix-it" strategies are equal. There are usually multiple strategies to draw upon depending on the type of change you are considering. For example, to fix a leaky pipe, field crews will close off a valve or "squeeze" the line if necessary; in the same way that a kink in a garden hose to stop the water flow.

Some people speak before thinking. As it applies to your career, squeezing the line is the equivalent of biting your tongue when you say something toxic or harmful to others or yourself. This strategy is like applying a tourniquet to stop the bleeding.

Other times, a section of pipe is so corroded or damaged that it needs to be cut out and replaced with a new pipe or fitting. A key skill is to know when to turn off your valve when a sensitive situation emerges. You may need to replace old habits with new, healthier behaviors that will better serve your career needs and help you to achieve your goals. While biting your tongue can be effective, the initial energy or impulse is still there. It's a band-aid, and band-aids have a way of falling off. The time, cost, and effectiveness of different strategies vary. In this vein, it is important to be mindful of the short and long-term solutions that apply to your career leaks.

Similarly, the efficiency of the strategies you choose to help you start a new career, or to enhance your existing career, each come with their own pluses and minuses. For example, in many teams I work with there is often someone who is technically superb, a strong performer who gets things done, but at the heavy cost of burning bridges with people along the way. As part of your own recovery plan you can conduct a "relationship audit" and take subsequent steps to mend relationships with people you burned in the past. A relationship audit requires you to have your eyes wide open and involves some raw honesty with yourself with a combination of self-awareness and emotional intelligence.

Emotional intelligence involves an awareness of how what you say and do affects relationships with others. It also involves being able to effectively manage your relationships. You may need to check in with others to solicit feedback about where you stand with them when you suspect things are not as strong as they ought to be.

Managing your career takes a great deal of attention and effort over the long-term. Think about how you will recover from any career missteps that you already made. Learning about what caused your leaks and explosions and how to recover, how to repair them, enables you to move forward.

The next chapter focuses on how you can manage and maintain your own system of pipes so that they stay in shape and help sustain you along your career journey.

Questions to consider:

- What career mistakes have you made?
- If someone conducted a relationship audit on you or about you, what might they find?
- What are some options for you to repair any damaged relationships?

You don't repair that relationship by sitting down and talking about trust or making promises. Actually, what rebuilds it is living it and doing things differently - and I think that is what is going to make the difference.

- Patricia Hewitt, British politician

MAINTAINING YOUR NETWORK OF PIPES

I can't change the direction
of the wind, but I can adjust my
sails to always reach my destination.

- Jimmy Dean, Country music
singer and businessman

Just as pipeline operators continually check and maintain the pipes in a natural gas system, you can check and maintain aspects of yourself and your career. Creating and consistently maintaining healthy personal habits is important for helping ensure that you retain a state of balance, longevity, and quality experiences during your career.

Last time I checked, none of us is a "fusion factory" where we can generate energy and productivity for eternity! It becomes evident that a key challenge is to find a way to consistently perform well and remain passionate and engaged at work. If you consistently take good care of yourself throughout your career, you will have the energy and capacity needed to appropriately tend and sustain a satisfying career in the long run.

SELF-MAINTENANCE

Just as there are different pipe sizes and materials in a natural gas system and they all fit and work together to perform a job, your personal set of pipes work together to perform a job, too. Many modern pipeline systems have valves that automatically shut the flow of gas to a home or business during earthquakes which protects the pipes and the community from serious harm. You may be more familiar with a circuit breaker that cuts off electrical surges that can overwhelm a circuit's capacity to handle it.

Letting yourself get to the point of overwhelm, burnout, and dissatisfaction is like a flashing warning sign telling you activate your shutoff valves, assess the scene, and plan a new route that aligns better with your personal vision for your work and life.

There are two main approaches that pipeline operators use to maintain their equipment and keep their operations running smoothly, and you can consider them for maintaining your own well-being and career. One approach is to have scheduled maintenance programs such as setting new goals at the beginning of each year and evaluating your progress halfway through the year. The other approach is referred to as a "condition-based" maintenance program.

With the scheduled approach, pipeline operators check valves periodically to make sure they operate properly and when necessary. This testing and maintenance is done at regular intervals such as monthly or quarterly.

Operators using the condition-based approach utilize sensors embedded in the system that inform them when an asset failure is about to occur or has occurred. Customers are excellent sensors. They serve as the eyes and ears for a gas utility and contact the company when there is something wrong with one of their gas appliances. For example, they will contact the company for assistance when they smell gas, their gas appliance stops working, or when they discover their heater is not working when the house gets too cold.

You have the equivalent available to you as well. What will signal to you that you are on-track or veering off-track? For some people, it is the feeling of being out of control, missing deadlines, having unresolved problems with work, withdrawing from participation in team meetings, or acting overly dominating and controlling. It's all personal. Be aware of the various signs that will let you know when an course adjustment is needed.

Determining your preferred type of maintenance program is a personal choice. Based on knowing yourself, you will have the best understanding of what may work best. You may find that a combination of both approaches is the most effective. Of course, the best maintenance program is the one that you consistently use.

The advantage of the scheduled approach is that each asset is assessed on a regular basis. The drawback is that sometimes the check-in times may be too late—after damage has been done—while at other times, the check-ins are more frequent than needed and may involve unnecessary maintenance costs. Therefore, if you regularly go to the gym or participate in some other form of exercise on certain days of the week, stick to scheduled eating and sleeping times, have annual check-ups at the doctor, etc. that is analogous to the traditional maintenance program.

The advantage of the condition-based maintenance approach is that assets are taken care of as needed and "just-in-time," and this avoids unnecessary maintenance costs while also sidestepping costly damages caused by malfunctioning or overtaxed assets. The drawback is that you may occasionally have a faulty sensor and miss the symptoms indicating that your attention is needed. Therefore, if you adjust your workout or exercise regimen each week based on what else you have going on, you only eat when you are hungry and abstain when you're not, sleep when you feel tired, and visit the doctor as often as you need to as symptoms arise, then that is analogous to having yourself on a condition-based program.

A key thing to remember is that you don't need to go on your career journey alone. Just as companies use teamwork in order to keep the pipeline system in top working order, building a strong social network for moral support on an ongoing basis can be your personal source of strength. Having partners to support you can be powerful and will help encourage and sustain you through the ups and downs of your journey. Examples of partners are your family, friends, clergy, counselors, and coworkers.

CAREER MAINTENANCE

You can use the elements of the **7 Pipelines of Career Success**™ model as a personal "Career Maintenance Checklist". The scheduled and condition-based maintenance principles discussed above equally apply to how you maintain your career.

CAREER MAINTENANCE CHECKLIST

MY PERSONAL PIPES	FREQUENCY
✓ PURPOSE & PASSION	EVERY 6 MONTHS
○ PREPARATION	
✓ PREFERENCES	EVERY 12 MONTHS
○ PRINCIPLES/VALUES	
○ PERSONALITY	
✓ PERFORMANCE	AS NEEDED
○ POTENTIAL	

Tending to your personal pipes on a regular basis will deliver dividends for you and your career. Regardless of the methods you choose to use, remember to be consistent. In fact, you may choose to go with a hybrid approach. An example would be check-ins with your boss and peers about your career goals at regular intervals while reaching out to them for immediate feedback whenever accomplishing a major milestone or experiencing a setback.

Unfortunately, you may realize there is a significant mismatch between your seven pipes and your current or prospective job opportunities. However, knowing when it's just not a right fit can be empowering. When a valve closes, you can open valves to new options. New networks of career possibilities outside the company that were previously unavailable to you become accessible.

The outcome of personal and professional changes is usually uncertain. There is a level of faith involved in sticking with it whether learning a new skill, trying on a new attitude, or starting a new job or career without assurances that things will work out as anticipated. There are powerful forces at play when you make your intentions explicitly known to yourself and others. Have faith that the career path that unfolds before you will lead you to where you wish to go. Your life's purpose is a means for living out your personal vision. Staying connected to your core passion-purpose pipe will keep you going and continually re-energize you throughout your journey.

Questions to consider:

- What sensors exist to let you know when your personal system is reaching its capacity?
- What methods do you use (or can you establish) to increase your ability to handle high-pressure situations effectively before shutting down occurs?
- What indicators exist to let you know when your career is on track or off track?
- What mechanisms can you put into place to maintain an ideal degree of satisfaction and progress in your career?

Is the system going to flatten you out and deny you your humanity, or are you going to be able to make use of the system to the attainment of human purposes?

- Joseph Campbell, American
mythologist and writer

CAREER CONTINUUM: YOUR FUTURE

The best way to predict your future is to create it.

- Abraham Lincoln,
Sixteenth U.S. President
who abolished slavery

A natural gas company certainly doesn't have a lock on the energy market. There are many alternative sources and distributors of energy that we use each day. Likewise, the concepts and ideas and I have put forward in this book are not the only source of career advice in the marketplace. Type in "career success" on Amazon alone and you can find more than 77,000 books on the topic.

What I wanted to do with this book was to draw upon my personal experience to stimulate and provoke your thinking about some core principles and key aspects of your career that are necessary to think about. My hope for you is that you'll remember the principles contained in the

7 Pipelines of Career Success™ model and apply them to your own career journey as you take your next steps and move forward from here.

Assuming you desire to be at a different place in your career at some point, the most important thing is to do *something*. Having gone through several career and job changes myself, I've found that it helps to enlist the support of others as well as to give back to others in need along the way. Just as it takes a community of committed employees to run a successful company, it is important that you enlist the support of your own community; your network of family, friends, and colleagues to assist you and help you hold yourself accountable for your career transition. If you don't have a strong network, become involved outside of your normal routine and work environment and begin to build one.

Your future success hinges upon a foundation of principles contained in *Pipe Dreams: 7 Pipelines of Career Success*. Taking charge of your own career can be daunting at times, yet incredibly liberating as well. It fuels your personal and professional growth, regardless of the outcome! Whether you make missteps, take detours, run around cul-de-sacs, or hit solid objects as you dig deep to get to where you want to go, consider it all to be part of your discovery process. If nothing else, take some basic steps. Here are some proactive things you can do:

- Take time for self-reflection to illuminate your passion and purpose.
- Assess your personal assets (talents, strengths, personality, etc.).
- Initiate a career conversation with your boss and your company's Human Resources representative.
- Request the support of your boss and peers and ask for feedback to uncover your blind spots.
- Demonstrate a positive attitude and a continuous desire to learn and grow.

Being clear about who you are, what you value, and what you're passionate about will generate a vital force that energizes you along the way, leading you to a more fulfilling and engaging career.

You have many choices ahead of you whether you are in the early, middle, or sunset stage of your career. Whatever path you take will lead you to new possibilities. As an employee, it is important to be mindful of acceptable and unacceptable practices within your company's culture. The benefit of making a career shift while working for your company is that you can draw upon your track record of performance, and benefit from a larger safety net to catch you while you are taking risks.

Things will certainly continue to evolve and change. Take comfort in knowing that you are capable and you have the necessary tools in your toolbox that equip you to better navigate the routes ahead and form new chapters in the story of your career.

Do we really need to traverse all of Oz killing witches and whatnot to learn that we've had the power all along?

- Eliza Rhodes, Writer and philosopher, author of *Sign Language*

SELF-AWARENESS RESOURCES

It is not the mountain we conquer, but ourselves.

- Sir Edmund Hillary, New Zealand explorer among first to summit Mount Everest

There are different types of tools available that can help you become more aware of your strengths, interests, values, and interpersonal style and how you can improve your overall effectiveness. Someone in your company's HR department may offer some of these tools:

Assessment	Description	Comments
iStartStrong™ by CPP	Career interests	On-line self-assessment and personalized report *Available at CPP.com*
StrengthsFinder 2.0 by Tom Rath	Top five talents/strengths	Book with link to free on-line self-assessment and personalized report *Available at Amazon.com*
Birkman Method by Sharon Birkman-Fink & Stephanie Capparell	Personality, career interests, and leadership style	Book with link to free on-line self-assessment and personalized report *Available at Amazon.com*
Emotional Intelligence 2.0 by Travis Bradberry & Jean Greaves	Emotional intelligence	Book with link to free on-line self-assessment and personalized report *Available at Amazon.com*

Assessment	Description	Comments
DiSC Profile by Wiley/Inscape Publishing	Work/behavioral style, communication, strengths	On-line self-assessment and personalized report *Available at EverythingDiSC.com*
Meyers-Briggs Type Indicator (MBTI) by CPP	Personality style, communication, strengths	On-line self assessment and personalized report *Requires certified facilitator or coach*
360 degree feedback assessment	Obtain anonymous feedback about your strengths and development needs from boss, peers, (in)direct reports, customers/clients, vendors, and others	On-line multi-rater assessment and/or interviews conducted by neutral third party *Requires third party advisor such as coach or consultant*

Expecting opportunity to knock while you do nothing is like expecting to get milk by holding out a bucket.

- Ted Dreier, Author of
Moozie's Cow Wisdom

ACKNOWLEDGMENTS

This book is written for all career seekers and builders who strive to become their best selves, including all the hard-working SoCalGas employees and leaders who have shared their struggles and successes with me while inspiring me to write this book.

In any career it is always beneficial to have both mentors and mensches who impart a positive influence. I'd like to thank numerous individuals who have been instrumental throughout my own career journey and have impacted me in meaningful ways. I'd also like to give shout-outs to the many friends, family and colleagues who have supported me in the writing of this book.

My first mentors and role models were my parents, Irv and Barb Gellman. I am forever grateful for the freedom they granted me to explore and pursue my own dreams rather than prescribe more narrowly defined career paths as many well-intentioned parents do. I owe my strong work ethic to watching them model the way over a span of thirty-five years running family-owned businesses. My father was both a pharmacist and entrepreneur. While serving as a stock boy in my father's drugstore from the time I was eight years old, I learned about business fundamentals and the value of developing relationships with people of all economic circumstances, colors, and backgrounds. My mother was a nurse, entrepreneur, and community advocate. From her I learned the value of persistence and standing strong for what you believe in. She was a catalyst for change ahead of her time to bring better nutrition to schools.

I had another great mentor, Peggy Covert, while I was an undergraduate student at San Diego State University. She pushed me to take risks and provided me valuable opportunities to stretch beyond my comfort zone in order to grow as an aspiring Organizational Development professional. Peggy exemplified what it meant to have someone who believes in the best that others can be—even though I didn't always have the same level of self-confidence in myself as she had in me.

In my early years as an aspiring HR professional, Bonnie Burn was a great friend and mentor who opened up her home office and her classroom and allowed me to tag along and watch one of the most enthusiastic and best trainers in action. Ultimately, she helped me understand what it meant to be a dynamic trainer and classroom facilitator.

In graduate school at Springfield College, Dr. Barbara Mandell played an important role in my career development. Her caring nature, wisdom, and penchant for a timely laugh was a much needed tonic while I was a long way from home. It was under her guidance that I gained the practical skills and self-confidence to become a practicing consultant, trainer, and coach.

In my first job at the world-famous San Diego Zoo upon finishing graduate school, Alan Landers expertly helped guide me in thinking through and conducting my very first organizational client intervention. I fondly remember being at his house and laying out all the variables on a long piece of butcher paper and post-it notes.

Over the years, Doug Walker was a welcome respite during intermittent career transitions. He was a great sounding board and champion for keeping my spirits up and keeping me focused. Our rich, after-hours conversations were especially treasured.

Jane Valentine, Brienn Woods, and Mo Mouton were among the best managers I ever had and were instrumental in my maturation as an Organizational Development professional during my time with Sempra Energy's utilities (both SDG&E and SoCalGas). They modeled the way with their character, competence, ethics, and kindness. I am forever indebted to Jane for her humanity and for teaching me that sometimes "good is good enough" whenever I got bogged down in my never-ending quests for perfection. Brienn was a brilliant and phenomenal partner as both a peer and mentor whose creative genius left me in awe and introduced me to new ways to elevate my game in my work. Mo was the consummate boss for his steadfast encouragement, acknowledgement, path clearing and faith which enabled me to pursue my passion for coaching and successfully bring it to life for SoCalGas employees. I'm also indebted to Jimmie Cho, a true mensch, who as my Vice President went out of his way to demonstrate care and concern during a difficult period of organizational change and my personal transition.

My mentor coach of the past two years, the fabulous Michael Stratford, possesses an unrivaled mastery of the metaphor. His musings tickled my imagination and provided extra inspiration to me during the most recent stage of my career journey. Michael continually provided encouragement, support, advice and ceaselessly challenged me to apply the principles I was writing about in my book to "live" situations I was experiencing at work. This was profoundly impactful to me. Thanks for keeping me honest and helping me evolve as a transformative professional, sensible parent, and authentic author along the way.

There were also numerous individuals who played an active role in my writing journey. I'd like to thank Maggi Kirkbride, my grand editor, who is the reason this book only costs about $15 instead of $100. She adopted the voice of the reader and gently nudged me to do away with extravagantly "expensive" words and overly-technical explanations that often behooved me to buckle down and simplify. Maggi's sense of humor and willingness to try different approaches and grow with me is something that I appreciated along the way (especially during growing pains). Thank you Maggi for sharing your wonderfully eccentric and enigmatic life with me. A hat tip also goes out to Sarah McArthur who provided initial editorial feedback when I finished my first draft.

My fabulous graphic designers, Kendra Heard and Adan Garcia, were able to magically translate my hazy visions into concrete realities that captured the essence of what I wanted to convey to my readers. Both of them went above and beyond expectations, and I am grateful for having such a visually appealing book that invites readers to dive in and discover.

My subject matter experts, Cedric Williams and Ed Banuelos, gave up many hours of their own time to help ensure my Pipeline model, gas industry anecdotes and analogies were on the mark and had "street credibility." I also appreciated the assist by Hugo Mejia for sharing his perspective on my Pipeline model and providing me with ideas for tweaking the design.

I am thrilled that Anne Smith, an admired and beloved former Chairman and CEO of SoCalGas, graciously agreed to write the foreword to my book when I approached her prior to her retirement. She truly exemplifies the hallmarks I discuss in this book as mirrored by her own career path.

A special thanks goes out to my closest friends. Adam Davush (Davushky!) lent a hand with his artistic skills and helped bring my Pipeline model to life two years ago after our brainstorm meeting. My dear friend, Roberto Weinstein, gave me some brutally honest feedback upon reviewing my first and subsequent drafts. I must confess it was hard to swallow at the time, but in the end it spurred me on to dig deeper to make this a book that all employees can enjoy, understand and apply. I also appreciated the ongoing encouragement that my friend, Greg Benusa, provided along the way.

I am also grateful to my awesome Review Team (including my friends and subject matter experts named above) of Doris Sims, Mo Mouton, and Guy Morin. They scoured my final draft and provided me with valuable feedback for finishing touches to give my book the best possible chance of success in helping my readers.

Finally, I am delighted to have benefitted from the help of my brilliant and perceptive son, Jonas, who at only ten years old, served as an invaluable partner by providing constructive feedback to help ensure my readers would readily understand my graphics. His interest in my book, listening to my ups and downs during the writing and editing process, and understanding of my many hours working late into the night only to be a groggy (and sometimes grumpy) Dad the next day, was a tremendous gift.

ABOUT THE AUTHOR

Mike Gellman is a Sr. Talent Management Advisor with the Southern California Gas Company (SoCalGas®). He has a Master's degree in Industrial/Organizational Psychology and is a graduate of an internationally accredited coach training program. Mike has devoted his career to helping individuals, teams, and organizations work more effectively and achieve their potential. He is passionate about training and coaching others to lead satisfying careers.

Over the past fifteen years, Mike has successfully facilitated numerous succession planning, leadership development, and organizational change initiatives in both corporate and nonprofit environments. Mike created an award-winning mentorship program for the San Diego chapter of the Association for Talent Development that has been running strong for over fourteen years. He also pioneered an innovative Career Self-Discovery program for SoCalGas and most recently launched a full-service Career Coaching & Development Center to assist employees in making career choices that play to their strengths and passions.

In addition to being a devoted dad of a bright ten-year-old son, Jonas, Mike enjoys hiking, camping, photography, running, and volunteering in his community. Born and raised in Cleveland, Ohio and having spent most of his professional career in San Diego, California, he currently resides in Irvine, California.

For a complimentary Personal Journal Guide to use along with this book, go to www.7pipelinesofcareersuccess.com

Five percent of all sales of this book will be donated to charities providing career-related support services to individuals in need.

For inquiries contact Mike at mike@mikegellman.com

39358288R00139

Made in the USA
San Bernardino, CA
24 September 2016